A Dream of Becoming

Nicole Dake

Published by Nicole Dake, 2024.

A DREAM OF BECOMING

First edition. December 2, 2024.

ISBN: 979-8230240112

Written by Nicole Dake.

Introduction

This book was written during my first year in Germany, where I moved from the US. This is a collection of poems about the ups and downs of moving into a new life.

This year, I am also exploring my spirituality, so some of the poems here speak to my spiritual journey as well.

It is a blending of new life, letting go, and jumping into something exciting and new. I hope that these poems will touch you if you are going through a life transition, or if you can relate to going through one.

A Message From the Angels

Image by Pixabay

My dearest
your angel has a message
just for you
for this new year
to help you find your way
through this world
to help you find your place
when you are
feeling so lost
You aren't lost
my beautiful one
you have the heart

of an angel yourself
and inside that heart
you know the way
you know the Truth
you know
all the things to say
You have to open
your heart to love
to kindness
and to friendship
Be more of yourself
instead of always less
be more of your heart
and less of your doubting mind
free your spirit
from the sands of time
and become your truth
remember how to fly
and you will go far
with wings in the sky
Become all you are
shed the illusions
of being less
than worthy
you are worthy
you are enough
you are bright
inside
your beautiful heart
Remember where
you come from
remember

what you need to do
remember
that life is less
about doing than being
You are called
human beings
for a reason
not human doings
remember that
You are worthy
just for being
who you really are
You are worthy
of love and light
you are worthy
of peace
you are worthy
of knowing the truth
you are worthy
of all the beauty
that life has to offer
just for *being* you

Are there People who Don't Have a Dream

Photo by Alex Azabache[1] on Unsplash[2]

Are there people out there

who don't have a dream?
Who don't have a fire inside
saying you have to do this?
How do you go through life
without fire and passion
and just content yourself
to go quietly to and fro
blown around like a leaf
without a clear direction?
Are there people like that?
Are there people who just
let life happen to them?
Are there people who don't think
what is coming tomorrow
who don't have this all-consuming
passion to do *something?*
whatever that something may be?
It feels like giving up to me
not to have some kind of dream
some kind of passion
some kind of direction
where you desperately want to go
how do you live like that?
doesn't it just feel empty?
How do you live with no passion?
shoveling down scoops of ice cream
with no thought for tomorrow
no thoughts of a dream?
I have always had dreams
I have always had goals

---

1. https://unsplash.com/@alexazabache?utm_source=medium&utm_medium=referral

2. https://unsplash.com?utm_source=medium&utm_medium=referral

or at least something that
I badly wanted to escape from
And escapism
is a form of nihilism and death
to be sure but it is an active
wish for death not
a passive acceptance
that you have died already
while you yet live
How do you live
when you don't have a dream
how are you so complacent
I would just start to scream
with pain and panic
a lack of true passion
Are there dreamers and then
everyone else?
Are there people who just
accept whatever fate hands them?
How do they live like that?
how do they content themselves
with just surviving another day
with some Netflix and chill
Don't you dream of love?
don't you dream of achievement?
Don't you dream of making a difference?
don't you at least dream of something?
How do you live with nothing
concrete to envision in front of you?
Doesn't it make you sad?
How do you live this way
like with blinders on

and going slowly forward
like lemmings toward
the edge of a cliff
without even caring
what is coming next?
I wish for you that
you would find a dream
that you would find something
that makes your soul feel alive
that makes you alive with passion
that makes you want to thrive
instead of just plodding along
being barely alive

Awake Before the Sun

Photo by Mohamed Nohassi[1] on Unsplash[2]

We awake before the sun
to a quiet world
a world asleep
and it feels dreamlike
surreal and peaceful
sitting alone in the darkness
as my family sleeps
I rise before the sun

1. https://unsplash.com/fr/@coopery?utm_source=medium&utm_medium=referral

2. https://unsplash.com?utm_source=medium&utm_medium=referral

stretch my arms to the sky
in Sun Salutation
it should be moon salutation
for as dark as it is today
The world sleeps
and I rise to dream
to write
to speak these words
into the silence
of the early morning
Speak words of affirmation
looking in the mirror
give myself words of love
as church bells begin to ring
and the stillness is shattered
Time to wake up now
the bells tell the world
time for you to shine

Awakening

Photo by bruce mars[1] on Unsplash[2]

Awakening
to the true nature
of our being
of our oneness
Oneness
with all that is

1. https://unsplash.com/@brucemars?utm_source=medium&utm_medium=referral

2. https://unsplash.com?utm_source=medium&utm_medium=referral

all that was
all that will be
Oneness through love
awakening from fear
becoming perfect peace
This is how we are
supposed to live
Living in oneness
living in love
peace and harmony
with all other beings
For we are all just part
of this vast whole
just cells
in the body of Life
We are all angels
here in human form
forgetting for a time
that truly we can fly
Remember
who you really are
where you come from
and where you return to
Then you will know
the opening of your heart
to the truest, purest love
that you can imagine
That love is your nature
flowing from your heart
back to yourself again
Remember your oneness
and you will become

more of yourself each time
that you breathe in the extasy
of just being alive
Remember your love
remember your light
remember who you are

Beginning to Age

Photo owned by author
When do we begin to accept
that the part of our lifes
that was good is over
You see these lines

on your face in the mirror
starting to form on your eyes
on your mouth
and you buy all
these creams to make you
look young again
Youth is seen as beauty
but with age comes wisdom
can't wisdom be beautiful too?
It makes me wonder when
I am going to stop living
my life
and just exist
Do you stop caring
about yourself
stop caring about
living your life
stop caring about
what comes next
Do you stop setting goals
stop moving forward
and just sit stagnant
waiting for inevitable death?
I don't want to live that way
I don't want to die that way
I want to be filled with meaning
with purpose and beauty
every day of my life
until my last
I want to embrace each morning
sit on my mat for yoga
breathe in peace and patience

exhale all that doesn't serve me
I want to live each day
with a sense of purpose
knowing there is still
something left to accomplish
How do we live fully
each day until our last?
How do we keep our fire alive
buring within our chest
every day when it seems
maybe futile
like there is no future
as good as our past
Do we look back with regret
at things left undone
from when we were young
or do we look forward
and say today is the day
that I am going to do this
Some people take up things
like sky diving
some people keep working
on a passion project
some people keep healing
all of the wounds within
and bring healing to others
with the knowledge that they gain
I see people aging
all around me
and aging differently
How do you decide
today is the day

that my life is over?
How do you decide
that you are going to give up?
Is it a conscious choice
or just bit by bit
you give things up
that matter the most
then you can't get them back?
How do you hold on
to a sense of meaning
to a sense of purpose
when the face in the mirror
stops looking like the person
that you have known all your life
Do you keep going
do you keep pushing
how do you stay strong
enough to keep going
when your body is tired?
How do you keep your mind
awake and alive inside
of a body that is aging
is it inevitable that you give up?
I don't want to give up
I don't want to just fade
away quietly in the night
I want to keep passion and fire
alive inside my soul
so that I can live
for the rest of my life
I don't want to just exist
without a sense of meaning

I want to really live
How do you keep going
how do you keep moving
always forward
though time takes its hold
over you?
I want to keep going
I want to live.

Bouncing Back

Photo by Sydney Sims[1] on Unsplash[2]

These days I bounce
back more quickly
still sad
but for less time
finding some rhythm
to my rhyme
Finding some reason
to still the madness

1. https://unsplash.com/@fairytailphotography?utm_source=medium&utm_medium=referral

2. https://unsplash.com?utm_source=medium&utm_medium=referral

finding ways to calm
the beast inside me
I want to go home
to somewhere lost
and I don't know
where that is
still not settled here
but nowhere to go
back to either
my home is gone
and I need to make
a new home here
I need to find
my place
Somehow out of time
and I feel like
everything is moving
so slowly
and I should adjust
I should fit here
in this new home
making acquaintances
who may become friends
again only time
can tell the answers
Sometimes I feel
like I am always waiting
for time to catch up
with my needs and
my racing mind
Too slow
too fast

I never know how
I am moving
all this illness
inside my brain
and I begin to feel
all of this pain
I can't hold it back
I can't make it go
But I bounce back
more quickly
these days
Less depressed
Less anxious
less filled with dread
less tears cried
But still I do cry
trying to find balance
trying to find my place
where is my place?
is it here?
somewhere near?
somewhere far?
And the dreaded question
is it anywhere?
do I even belong?
How do you create
a sense of belonging somewhere?
when you feel a stranger
a prisoner
inside your own mind?
I need to find quiet
I need to find stillness

something to quiet
all these angry voices
my voice now
mingled with voices
from the past
and I want to break free
Troubled thoughts
troubled mind
but it passes it seems
more quickly now and
I bounce back
faster this time
but tired
of all this bouncing

Brain Fog

Photo by Uday Mittal[1] on Unsplash[2]

It feels like my mind
isn't mine anymore
stuck in this fog
like I have fallen
to the bottom of a well
Everything feels far away
and hard to find
hard to focus

---

1. https://unsplash.com/@mittaluday?utm_source=medium&utm_medium=referral

2. https://unsplash.com?utm_source=medium&utm_medium=referral

though I have the time
It's like my mind
has flown away
somewhere
hiding inside me
I know
but hard to find
Feeling unwell
feeling sad
Makes my mind feel
trapped inside
a prisoner
locked in time
Waiting to feel better
waiting to reclaim myself
from the hands of time
waiting for thoughts
to flow again
I hate the waiting
I hate this feeling
like a prisoner
like my life isn't mine

Constant Evolution

Photo by NASA[1] on Unsplash[2]

We are all in a state
of constant evolution
growing and changing
We are not the same
as we were yesterday
or will be tomorrow
Each day we grow
each day we learn

1. https://unsplash.com/@nasa?utm_source=medium&utm_medium=referral

2. https://unsplash.com?utm_source=medium&utm_medium=referral

each day we are stronger
braver and wiser
A tree grows tall
an inch at a time
so do we grow
one day at a time
So do we walk
one step at a time
ever forward
on this journey of ours
Always in motion
always alive with
kinetic energy
that flows through
all life
And we move slowly
at first then quickly
when we learn our way
Always moving forward
we know not where
towards spiritual realization
of deeper secret truths.

Dissolve Your Fears

Photo by Herbert Goetsch[1] on Unsplash[2]

Dissolve yourself
into the oneness
dissolve your fears
dissolve your anger
dissolve your sadness
Remember your love
remember your light
the essence of who you are

1. https://unsplash.com/@hg_photo?utm_source=medium&utm_medium=referral

2. https://unsplash.com?utm_source=medium&utm_medium=referral

you are the oneness
You are all that is
all that was
all that will be
You are a piece of the universe
a drop of water in this ocean of life
When you fall from the sky
you are alone
but you return to the ocean
and you are in the oneness again
Apart, together
apart, together
This is how our lives flow
sometimes we forget
our true nature
when we are separate
then we remember
when we come together
This is how our life flows
this is what our heart knows
We are a part of all life
flowing home together

Do You Want to be a Lucky Girl?

Do you want to be a lucky girl?
do you want to live your best life?
do you want happiness
prosperity, and success
in love and in life?
Be a lucky girl with me

---

1. https://www.megapixl.com/anpet2000-stock-images-videos-portfolio
2. https://www.megapixl.com/

do the things
that set you free
do things that set
your heart and mind
on fire with light
Do things that scare you
do things that make
you scream out loud
with all the joy
in the world
Every day is a new day
every day is a new chance
to live the life of your dreams
all you do is join the dance
You can live your best life
you can dance through
the forest in the trees
you can walk in nature
next to silent streams
Life is beautiful
if we allow it to unfold
the way it wants to go
the way it wants us to go
We have to follow the path
aligned to our highest good
the path the universe
has laid out for us
here on this Earth
We want so many things
and the universe wants us
to have all of them and more
we just have to open up

and see our glowing potential
see our radiant selves
like the stuff of dreams
Life is the stuff of dreams
it is all you want and more
it is so beautiful and
you are so lucky
to be alive in this world
to have a chance at freedom
a chance at dreams come true
You can make your dreams
into your reality
if you shift your mindset
if you live your dreams
if you walk the path
the universe has for you
All the things you want
and more are already yours
you just have to claim them
to reach out towards the stars
and make your dreams ignite
make yourself more alive
Meditate, pray, dance, dream
This is the stuff that stars
are made of
all this energy created
from the fabric of time
is also in you and
you just have to claim it
call out to it deep
inside yourself and
find your higher purpose

This is how you get all
your dreams to come true
by living your highest good
and speaking your highest truth
You become the best version
of yourself today and every day
when you allow your dream life
to come into your real life
you can cross those rainbows
and dance with those unicorns
and laugh in the face of time
when you live your best life

Dream Another Dream

Photo by Hulki Okan Tabak[1] on Unsplash[2]

Dream another dream
dance another dance
breathe life
into your soul
do the things
that make you whole
Live forward
only glancing back occasionally
don't be so afraid
of things in the past
look for something
you know will last
Circle faster

1. https://unsplash.com/ja/@hulkiokantabak?utm_source=medium&utm_medium=referral

2. https://unsplash.com?utm_source=medium&utm_medium=referral

enjoy the dance
let your feet fly
as your spirit
to the wind
will come at last
whirling faster
your arms
your hair
and your life
moving quickly past
Enjoy your life
it is your dance
enjoy each moment
and let yourself
be free to fly
like the wind
like the stream
you move rhythmically
Flowing forward
not moving back
though you may go
the same path again
you aren't going back
to where you came from
your home is still your home
but you return changed

Facing Forward, Towards the Light

Photo by Sourabh Barua[1] on Unsplash[2]
Live your life

facing forward
towards the light
casting your shadow
backward into the night
Face away
from your fears
live your life for
those you hold dear
Let the lies of the past
stay back in the past
Set your eyes forward
towards the lights
in the night sky flying
Thousands of stars
strings of floating lanterns
and all of the lights
that guide you home
Look always ahead
lest you stumble
at an obstacle
in your path
looking backwards
into the past and
things you can't change
You can only change now
you can only change you
And anything else
is just an exercise
in futility

---

1. https://unsplash.com/@iamsourabh?utm_source=medium&utm_medium=referral

2. https://unsplash.com?utm_source=medium&utm_medium=referral

Falling in Love With Life

© Rebelml[1] | Megapixl.com[2]

Some will fall in love with life and drink it like a fountain, pouring like an avalanche, coming down the mountain. ~Butthole Surfers
Falling in love with life again
falling in love with myself
this person I have become

---

1. https://www.megapixl.com/rebelml-stock-images-videos-portfolio
2. https://www.megapixl.com/

on the other side of the fire
I am strong
I am brave
I am wise
I am older now and know
a little bit more about life
enough to admit
that I know far from everything
I am this tiny speck floating
across the vast sky
of the universe
I am a grain of sand
at the edge of the ocean
I am a cell in the giant body
that is all of existence
Wrinkles crease my face now
from smiling or frowning though
I don't actually know
I only have three expressions
happy, sad and mad
so one of the made those lines
And I try all these creams to
try to erase them
But I love my body
I love myself
every day
I start the morning with yoga
to feed myself and my soul
I write
these tiny couplets
to myself
for myself

And take you along
for the ride
Do you love yourself now?
are you in love with the person
staring back at you in the mirror?
you should be.
You are with yourself more
that you are with anyone else
and you know yourself better
than they ever will
You know what makes
your heart come alive
you know what makes
your soul wander free
Out there somewhere
is a dream you are chasing
but right here, right now
there is you
You are beautiful
you are bright
you shine
you are enough
Your life should be overflowing
with love for the person you are
the person you are becoming
the things that you do
every day
Every little thing in your day
should be aligned to your goodness
should be feeding your light
should make you feel good
about just being you

I am falling in love that way
with my authentic self
chipping away the layers
of all the things that aren't me
all the things that aren't serving
my highest divine good
Let them slip away
like dust from my fingertips
all those negative thoughts
all the judgement from
other people
all the norms of society
that tell you how to be
average
I don't want to be average
I don't want to be normal
I don't want to be boring
and I don't need to fit
I want to dance in the rain
and in the sunshine
to feel it warm on my face
to spin around and around
to laugh with pure freedom
I want to show my true face
the one that hid behind
a mask for too long
I want to wear these clothes
I want to like the things I do
I want to feel comfortable
inside my own skin
because no one else
has to live here, just me

And inside myself
I feel safe to be me
I feel safe to open up
I feel safe to be free

Feeling Pensive Today

Photo by Guillaume Bolduc[1] on Unsplash[2]

1. https://unsplash.com/@guibolduc?utm_source=medium&utm_medium=referral

Do you sometimes
feel a bit pensive
and contemplate
everything
the nature of existance
the nature of yourself?
I feel that way today
like I am journeying inward
looking for answers
or maybe just the right
questions
If you ask the wrong question
the answer makes no sense
the answer to life, the universe and everything
is 42
But what is the ultimate question
that this answer is telling us 42
is the answer to?
Yeah a bit of
Hitchhiker's guide
for you this morning
It mocks everything
we try to understand
but is trying to understand
the mysteries
in itself a mockery?
Our minds are small
and time and the universe
so vast
All our minds are spinning
thinking thoughts so fast

2. https://unsplash.com?utm_source=medium&utm_medium=referral

How do we know the answer?
How do we know the question?
Just be open in your mind
open in your hands
open in your soul
and you will receive
the answers to oneness
somehow
Is it just a feeling?
I have felt it
Is it love?
I have felt that too
Are the questions we ask
answered in the wrong way
when we answer with
our minds?
Should we be asking
our hearts instead?
instead of always thinking
always in our head
The heart knows differently
it knows things quietly
without speaking them
because the heart
doesn't understand words
it only understands feelings
and our words for feelings
are woefully lacking
It is hard to express
a concept like love
in just one word
Hard to express oneness

in any words at all
they say,
Those who know do not speak. Those who speak do not know. ~Lao Tsu
So I am speaking and
that means that still
for all my seeking I
still do not know
the ultimate, vast answer
to that big question
that we all ask.
What is the meaning of life?

Finding Inspiration

Photo owned by Author

Where do you find inspiration?
Art imitating art
imitating life
it is all circular
things that make you feel alive
The feel of sunshine
on your face
the feel of the ocean
on your skin

the sand
beneath your feet
walking down the beach
in and out of waves
watching the endless ocean
at play
The ocean is ancient
ever the same
yet ever changing
it renews itself
with the cycle of water
it grinds mountains
to sand
with the passing of years
the landscape changes
volcanoes form islands
from beneath the waves
storms can crash ships
creating new sunken wrecks
ever changing
ever moving
the waves beat against the shore
Time moves us all
ever passing
ever moving
like grains of sand
through the hourglass
and we find ourselves
entranced by it all
Where do you find inspiration?
everywhere my lovelies
everywhere.

Defining Ourselves

Why are we on this journey
of finding ourselves?
are we lost?
aren't we right here?
Maybe we need a map
to tell us where *here* is

---

1. https://www.megapixl.com/undrey-stock-images-videos-portfolio
2. https://www.megapixl.com/

I am no different from you
and yet I am
this face this heart
my soul
But we are all parts
of the boundless soul
the boundless Self
that is the universe
pieces of each other
pieces of you
pieces of me
pieces of someone else
yet we are all the same
One heart that beats
in each chest
we are in our place
so what do we need to find?
An answer perhaps
too vast
to find the question to ask
And I just wonder
when I look at your face
a stranger's face
why do I see something
different?
Maybe we are on a journey
to find our sameness
instead of a unique identity
and I just wonder
at the meaning
of the boundless Self
We are all strangers

walking this way together
but the path is a circle
that takes us back home
to where we began
in a place without time
in a place we forgot
when we came to this world
How do we remember
how do we forget
how do we become
who we were meant to be
Are we already?
Aren't we already unfolding
like a beautiful
thousand-petaled lotus
We look for answers outside
instead of inside
but with my pen
here I sit exploring
the inner world
the world of the mind
the world of the soul
We dream
and perhaps there
we find our truth
What do we want?
We all want the same things
to love
to be loved in return
survival
exploration
the sun on our faces

We have made it too complicated
enforced our separation
but it is time to come home
to each other
time to come home
time to remember
where we came from
in that place beyond the stars
the place where we were one
and we yet dreamed

Finding Your Way Through the Darkness

Photo by Jackson Hendry[1] on Unsplash[2]

The night is like a vast
sleepless mother
who cares for us
as we sleep
as we dream
free from the pressures
of the waking world
Sometimes we wake to a new day

1. https://unsplash.com/@actionjackson801?utm_source=medium&utm_medium=referral
2. https://unsplash.com?utm_source=medium&utm_medium=referral

afraid
of what is yet to be
other times
free and full of purpose
ready to see
what comes next
Our hearts are fragile
if our intentions are pure
and we can be hurt by love
by loss of that love
and by our own expectations
when they go unmet
Sometimes we can move forward
with love and confidence
other times we stumble onward
driven only by fear
Yet at all these times
we find the vastness
of the stars above
and we glance upward
to make our silent wish
Our hearts all have wishes
when we are quiet enough
to hear them
we all have dreams
of something more inside us
We gaze up at the moon
with its magic
and its mystery
wondering if this light
in the darkness
will light our way forward

At night the stillness speaks
out of the darkness of our souls
asking us questions
that daylight cannot reach
and we search
for something in ourselves
to answer back
something to make sense
of the vastness of space
Are we really alone
on this little blue planet
or is there other life
somewhere far away
It is easy to feel small
when we gaze at the vastness
of that night sky
Our own smallness
can be comforting
make us realize
that the answers we seek
aren't so vast after all

Freedom of Choice

Photo by Luca Bravo[1] on Unsplash[2]

Freedom to choose
we always have it
yet seldom
do we leave our routine
we do what we do
often out of habit
without thought
of trying something new

1. https://unsplash.com/@lucabravo?utm_source=medium&utm_medium=referral

2. https://unsplash.com?utm_source=medium&utm_medium=referral

New year
new you
and we move forward
trying to find change
trying to find ourselves
a new version of me
in 2023
That is what we are seeking
that is what we are finding
somewhere in the mists
shrouding the dark road
Road less traveled
and we have to trust
in where it will lead
to somewhere unseen
far ahead in the trees
We will go somewhere
new and beautiful
but afraid of pitfalls
and the wind on my face
telling me to go back
go home
go somewhere safe
But safety breeds boredom
and we need to be free
need to try something new
need to be brave
and wander into somewhere
out in the unknown
Out there waits adventure
out there waits answers
to questions long silent

within my heart
feeling the stillness
of my breath in the cold
and I walk onward
on this new path
to see where it leads
To the place of my dreams?
our dreams lie in wait
on the other side of fear
near and far
this is where we go
See where the new path leads
somewhere in the dense trees
somewhere, somewhere, somewhere
Where does the path less traveled lead?
Somewhere on the other
side of all my fear

Getting up When You Fall

Photo by Vidar Nordli-Mathisen[1] on Unsplash[2]

Sometimes in life
we fall down
but we have to
get back up
It is hard to pull
yourself up by the bootstraps
one more time
out of the mud

1. https://unsplash.com/@vidarnm?utm_source=medium&utm_medium=referral

2. https://unsplash.com?utm_source=medium&utm_medium=referral

but we have to
We need to remember
all the goodness of life
and a reason
to keep on going
after our fall
Of course
falling hurts
and we wish that someone
would help us up
but sometimes
we have to try
to pull up ourselves
We need to be the strong person
for ourselves so often
instead of having a hand to hold
We need to pull ourselves up
we have to move ourselves forward
to make ourselves strong again
when we don't feel that way inside
Finding strength is hard
finding love is harder
so we need to be our own hero
we need to be our own love
We need to be our own cheerleader
and move our selves forward

Healer, Heal Yourself

Healer, heal yourself
walk your path
through the darkness
to find the light again
and to find your love
inside yourself
inside life's heart
Remember
where you came from
remember
why you came here
remember
what you are
supposed to do

---

1. https://www.megapixl.com/nikkizalewski-stock-images-videos-portfolio
2. https://www.megapixl.com/

This is your calling
this is your path
uphill sometimes
through the snow
Looking for goodness
and things not shown
Your way isn't easy
your healing isn't linear
you fall sometimes
you falter sometimes
but always
you pick yourself up
and on you go
with determination
pulling yourself forward
onward and upward
Towards the summit
of the mountain you go
the place of the mystic
the place of dreams
you follow your heart
no matter how hard it seems
You climb so far
searching for answers
searching for light
searching for god
and you find the face
inside your own heart
You traveled far
through these obstacles
to find your way back
to Self and Source

knowing now the answer
lies inside yourself
and it was hiding here
all along
The journey is about
peeling back the layers
Not about becoming
but about unbecoming
everything that wasn't you
You weren't meant to be more
you were meant to be less
of the things of the world
Your climb was about
leaving things behind
every mile you went up
you left the world behind
you left your loved ones
you left other travelers
who couldn't
complete the path
You found the way
you found the mountain
you climbed to the top
and you found
the mystic texts there
and it told you
the answer to yourself
the answer to the soul
And you found yourself
you found yourself here
hiding under all the layers

Healing and Peace

Photo by Tj Holowaychuk[1] on Unsplash[2]

Finding peace isn't easy
and trying to hold onto it
almost impossible
But eventually we realize
peace isn't meant to be held
it is our natural state of being
Peace is the quiet
background of our thoughts

1. https://unsplash.com/@tjholowaychuk?utm_source=medium&utm_medium=referral
2. https://unsplash.com?utm_source=medium&utm_medium=referral

Peace is the blank canvas
on which we paint
the bright stories of
our lives
Similarly healing is a process
and it doesn't happen overnight
Just like we put on a band-aid
for a child on their little cut
we put band-aids on
our broken hearts
then we wait for it to heal
Our bodies naturally heal
if enough time passes
so do our hearts and minds
if we let the band-aid and
the Neosporin do it's job
Leave the band-aid on
don't pick at the wound
don't let the air touch it
don't let the dirt get in
Sometimes we leave our wounds
open and gaping instead
and there are things always
touching them and tearing
them open all over again
That is why wounds need to be covered up
they need to be treated by a doctor or
a mommy who knows best
Wounds won't heal if we just leave
them there untreated
they start to scab over
but then they scratch open again

or get a nasty infection
if we don't take care of them
Even so, we should take care
of our broken hearts and minds
the way we do our bodies
we need to realize that they too
need proper treatment for healing
We can't just leave them bleeding
our hearts and our minds
and expect time to do the work
We have to put the healing work in
and it is so much easier
if we do it at the beginning
when the hurt first happens
instead of leaving
things uncovered to fester
to get torn open again
or get dirt stuck inside
We take care of our outer wounds
why not our inner wounds too?
Why do we think they will just
get better on their own
if we don't do some first aid
to treat them?
Our hearts are no less fragile
than our skin
our minds no less prone
to lingering infection
Let yourself get well
go get stitched up
at the doctor if you need it
don't be so proud that

you think you don't need
proper help to heal
Things take longer
to heal when left untreated
And an unhealed mind
can make for an
unhealed spirit and
unhealed relationships
We go around with this
gaping, festering wound
asking people to ignore it
telling them we are fine
pretending things are normal
but they are far from that
It takes time to find
healing and peace in
our minds after heartbreak
but we need to focus
at least a little time
on our healing
be like a child and
ask mommy for a band-aid

Homecoming

Photo by Beto Galetto[1] on Unsplash[2]
Time to come home
walk through the door

1. https://unsplash.com/@betogaletto?utm_source=medium&utm_medium=referral

2. https://unsplash.com?utm_source=medium&utm_medium=referral

look at the cats
sitting on the floor
This is my house
this is my home
though I have gone
the time has flown
Time passes by
taking us away
out in the world
to dream our dreams
live our lives
and sometimes
we are far away
from where we have grown
Time to come home
sweep out the corners
from the cobwebs
rediscover ourselves
make new routines
find new ways to feel
like we belong here again
There is so much
life we live at home
and so much outside
and life
is about finding balance
between the two

How Do I Set Myself Free

Of other people's unspoken expectations

Photo by Anna Samoylova[1] on Unsplash[2]

I feel as though pulled
100 different directions
do this do that
hurry do it faster
do it now
but which thing first
which priority?

1. https://unsplash.com/@hagalnaud?utm_source=medium&utm_medium=referral

2. https://unsplash.com/?utm_source=medium&utm_medium=referral

So many goals
dreams, hopes and aspirations
so many responsibilities
so many people who all
need something now
always now
no time to stop
just go
just hurry
Flitting to and fro
from this to that
from here to there
never get to finish
what I started first
just these restless
endless spurts
When is it time
for me time now
when do I get to be
the priority
don't ask me how
Why are other people's needs
more important than mine?
because they scream louder
inside my mind
I am screaming too
but quietly
locked in this silence
of words I don't say
it's not about me
it's about you
your needs and

your feelings
Your feelings are bigger
your feelings are louder
they scream from your very being
but I am quiet
just standing here
listening to everyone else
their words drown mine out
stay quiet
I am too good
at just staying quiet
When is it my turn
for my dream
when do I get what I want
I just want to scream
Key Message: To set yourself free you have to speak up. Sometimes that is impossibly hard.

How do You Feel

Photo by Nathan Dumlao[1] on Unsplash[2]

How do you feel

when strange things happen
each and every day
in each and every way
how do we know
how to feel
How do we know
what comes next
how do we know why
we feel as we do
each day
Sometimes there are triggers
in situations that happen
and it makes us feel sad
Sometimes something beautiful
happens and we feel glad
Happy, sad, glad, mad, loved
so many different feelings
and what we base them on
sometimes is so haphazard
We allow situations to control
all of our thinking
and all of our feelings
instead of controlling ourselves
We move in strange directions
in circumstances twisting and turning
We twist and turn ourselves
like puzzle pieces
that just don't fit
like this dance
in stop motion

1. https://unsplash.com/@nate_dumlao?utm_source=medium&utm_medium=referral

2. https://unsplash.com?utm_source=medium&utm_medium=referral

that doesn't go
where it is supposed to go
it feels forced
it feels wrong
And we learn how
to do something else
something different
something that fits
and something that flows
We have to learn to be free
from ourselves and circumstances
to self-determine our feelings
instead of letting ourselves
be controlled by everything
and anything

Hurt People, Hurt People

Photo by Adam Flockemann[1] on Unsplash[2]

Hurt people, hurt people
I know, I am one of them
hurt in so many ways
by the turns life takes
Yes, I know sometimes
I am a shit person
responding to the
shit circumstances
life has handed me
I know that's no excuse
I know I shouldn't get jealous
or so upset about things
but I am wired that way
wired to care too much
and get broken too easily
by things people say and do
I have been through too much
for things to always be easy
for me
I know that makes things hard
for you to be with me
I know that I hurt you
but you hurt me too
It isn't right the way
hurt people hurt others
we just don't know how
to react in a healthy way
all the time
especially when triggered
from trauma of the past

---

1. https://unsplash.com/@gal8xies?utm_source=medium&utm_medium=referral

2. https://unsplash.com?utm_source=medium&utm_medium=referral

I know it isn't an excuse
it is a reason
Did you know trauma
causes brain damage
I'm not normal like
you would like me to be
and though I can pretend
when times are good
when it gets bad I
go into fight or flight
and if you back me
into a corner then
I can't run and
I strike back
with everything I've got
I say things that are unkind
and downright hurtful
It isn't a good
way to react
I know that
I know that it isn't right
for hurt people
to hurt people
but deep inside me
something is broken
I don't know if it is ever
going to be fixable
But not when I am triggered
that's for sure
I can't live my whole life
in fight or flight
and expect to be nice

Maybe someday I won't be so hurt
and I can stop saying the things
that hurt people do
maybe someday I can stop
the screams inside my mind
the screams
that come from my lips
on the bad days
I want to heal
I want to get better
I want to be the bigger person
but I can't always
If you yell at me
if you back me in a corner
I'm going to come out swinging

I Write Sad Poems

From my sad heart

Photo by D A V I D S O N L U N A[1] on Unsplash[2]

I write little sad poems
from my sad heart
with bleeding little fingers
making broken art
A glass of wine
a pen
a window frame

---

1. https://unsplash.com/@davidsonluna?utm_source=medium&utm_medium=referral

2. https://unsplash.com?utm_source=medium&utm_medium=referral

staring into time
without any reason
just rhyme
So many things lost
things found
and I still here
still a fool after
all of this time
Broken heart
broken mind
and still somehow
going on forward
Time marches
we move like a dance
twisting this way and that
like a tree on the wind
Whispers of madness
silent tears
all these questions
ring in my ears
and I wonder
if I did right
choices, choices, choices
And I just wonder
if I chose right
or if it is possible
when you are pulled
by two halves of your heart
each going
a different direction
across a span of miles
across oceans

did I go the right way?
Can you every go the right way
when you leave half
of your heart behind?
Should I just focus now
on the part of my heart
that is right here?
Or is it impossible
to ignore the giant
gaping cut
where the other half
of my heart used to be
Yes I write sad poems
always sad poems
Somewhere in the verse
I find a measure of peace
of patience
sometimes answers
show their face
But not today.
Today has no answers
no right or wrong
because how do you choose
between two halves
of yourself?

Key Message: Sometimes it is okay to feel torn in half. Because you actually are.

Is it Fixable?

Photo by Motoki Tonn[1] on Unsplash[2]

The Japanese use gold
to fix broken cups
to make the pieces
whole again
like a mosaic
a painting made
from broken pieces
like a phoenix
risen from the ashes

1. https://unsplash.com/@motoki?utm_source=medium&utm_medium=referral
2. https://unsplash.com?utm_source=medium&utm_medium=referral

I know that you can
fix your broken pieces
back together again
into something beautiful
but today
right now
I am still just
a broken cup
Waiting to be fixed
by an artist's hands
It's like I am in a car wreck
by the side of the road
waiting for the rescue crew
to come and take me out
with the jaws of life
There are people
who fix broken things
so where is the person
who is going to come
and fix me?
Oh right.
when it comes to people
we are supposed to fix ourselves
"healer, heal thyself."
But how do you do that?
how do you fix what is broken?
when you have to do it
alone inside your mind
What do you do
when your mind itself
is what is broken?
I don't know if I have

strength left
to get up one more time
I don't know if I have
the willpower
to make myself
keep going
Why is it that
surrounded by people
I feel so alone
so hurt
so broken?
Why can't I feel
whole and healthy
like other normal people
my mind is the enemy
and I want to run away
but how do you run
away from yourself?
I need a potter
to fix my little broken cup
I need a doctor
to fix my broken mind
I need a lover
to fix my broken heart
I need someone
to make this pain go away
but deep inside I know
that someone is me
I need to become the potter
the doctor
the lover
to fit the broken pieces

back together
in a mosaic pattern
But right now
I am none of those things
I am just a
little broken cup

It's Time to Stand Up For Yourself

Photo by Drew Colins[1] on Unsplash[2]
It's time to stand up
for yourself

1. https://unsplash.com/@drewcolins?utm_source=medium&utm_medium=referral

2. https://unsplash.com?utm_source=medium&utm_medium=referral

your heart
your goodness
your dreams
Stop letting other people
define you
Stop letting them
tell you who you are
or who you should be
You are beautiful
you are bright
you are a shining
ray of light
Be who you are
who you want to be
who you are meant to be
instead of who they think
you are supposed to be
Be you
Be unapologetic
be strong
be fine
you are fine
you are strong
you are love
you are light and
you deserve to be free
So break free
of what other people think
and do what you think
do what you feel
follow your heart
and be real

Learning to Let Go

Photo by Alexandra Gorn[1] on Unsplash[2]
How do you learn
to be stronger than your fear

1. https://unsplash.com/@alexagorn?utm_source=medium&utm_medium=referral
2. https://unsplash.com?utm_source=medium&utm_medium=referral

to escape
those grasping hands
that clutch at you
from the darkness
How far away do you have to run
to be able to feel safe
when fear is all you have known
When is it time to go?
when is it time to run?
How do you know if staying
and fighting
will make a difference?
are you a match to the task?
will you win your fight?
How do you step
out of the darkness
and into the light
How do you know
if your cause is worthy?
if YOU are worthy?
when you have been told
so often that you aren't
The fear comes
from inside my own heart
and I cannot escape
the pain of the past
or the fear
of more pain to come
when I step right back
to where I was before
I just want to hide
crawl in bed

pull the blankets up tight
shut out the world
and its prying eyes
judging me
telling me I am not enough
How do you become enough?
for other people
not to hurt you?
Some people are strong
self-assured
but some of us
are frightened and vulnerable
hanging on
by barely a thread
to what little we have
fearing that too
will be taken away
All these strangers
taking up space
inside my mind
their voices scream
drowning out
the voice of my soul
tiny and quiet
telling me to try again
telling me to be brave
but it is there
my voice beneath the screams
I still have love
I still have dreams
Is the little bit
of strength I have

enough for one more fight?
is the little bit of light enough
to make it through the night?
Always endless questions
always endless fear
wondering when
will it become too much
I don't want to stay
knocked down this time
but I struggle
to get back up
struggle on fragile feet
bleeding hands
feelings of just
not enough
How do you become enough?
How do you become strong?
Keep fighting through the darkness
keep walking through the screams
persist in the face of danger
no matter how hard it seems
I have been the fighter
I have persevered
can I go on
just a little longer?
if I go just a little farther
will I find somewhere safe?
will I find an end to fear?
or does fear last forever
and we just have to keep
being brave
in spite of the things that hurt us

things we know are still
out there waiting in the darkness
as I sit here
in this tiny circle of light
cast by a single candle flame
How do we hold the darkness at bay?
how do we stumble forward?
Believing in fragile hope
that things could get better
get easier
or that we
could get stronger
I am tired of being strong
I am tired of being brave
I want someone to hold me
tight and keep me safe

Leave Your Blood on the Page

Photo by Dim Hou[1] on Unsplash[2]

When you are a writer
you put your heart
and soul in your words
yourself laid bare
out there for all to see
like being naked
in front of a crowd
your head held high

1. https://unsplash.com/@dimhou?utm_source=medium&utm_medium=referral

2. https://unsplash.com?utm_source=medium&utm_medium=referral

You put your life
and your thoughts
for all to see
in front of eyes
with your honesty
there for everyone
What if they judge you?
What if they hate it?
What if they leave terrible comments?
That's right
the comments section
it's love or hate
and you have to see
all of what they feel
when they read
what you felt
in the silence
of your heart
Letting your writing
out in the world
is like giving
your child a first car
it's freeing
but so dangerous
and you don't know
what is going on
what they want to do
what they want to see
what they want
for you to be
And we don't know
what people will say

So do you write for them
do you gear it to their needs
do you try to
people please?
or do you write your heart
do you lay it bare
let yourself bleed
red on the page?
How do you decide?
How do you find your truth?
We have these feelings
we don't want to offend
we don't want to be too much
or not enough
we want to be bright
and shining and happy
we want to make people
feel something beautiful
we want to make them
read something powerful
We want to be the best
we want to shine
like a diamond
up there in the sky
we want to make you dream
you have landed in the stars
We want to transport you
to the best in yourself
to make you dream a dream
of your best life
that you can feel
and see and taste it

we want to help you
to become that
the best in you
the part that shines
so you can be a diamond too
How can words do that?
How can they move the soul?
That is what writers want to do.
We want to touch you
make you feel something
of what we feel
we want to inspire you
to be like we are
we want you to be
dreamers too
for writers are always
dreamers
But we are dreamers
and doers at once
when we say these words
aloud into the silence
of the soul they speak
we want to move you
so you take some action
we want to help you
to make you dance
to help you love
to make you pure
and happy
and full of so much joy
full of romance
full of...

all the things you dream of
We want to speak
the silence of your souls too
that is our secret
We want your soul
to come alive
the way that ours does
when we write these lines
We want our words
to inspire your life
to make you come alive
more and more each day
We bravely walk the path
trying to pull you with us
so that you will speak
into the silence too
that you will open your veins
and bleed that red blood
onto the page too
We want you to live
an inspired life
the way we try
through our writing to do

Leaving You

There is a crushing weight on my soul
where you are supposed to be
my child
my heart
my soul
I cry out for you as if
in a dream you will come
you will be here
with me
like you are supposed to be
I didn't want to leave you
I wanted you with me
as a part of this new life
and it burns inside
this pain
Where you are supposed to be
right here
by my side
I cry for you
always and often
need you near
want you here
But you aren't here
you are so far away
and I see this empty room
that should be yours
filled with your voice and
your laughter
Everything reminds me of you
my whole life

tied up in raising you
and now
you are grown
and I am gone
and I blame myself
for leaving you
every day
every hour
every minute
This indescribable pain
the pain of you being so far away
Tears fall now
obscuring my vision
I miss you so much
it hurts inside
Yeah I am repetitive
all these thoughts
like a loop through my mind
asking how as a mother
I could leave you behind
How could I go out
in the world without you
how could I do this
how could I go
What kind of mother am I?
What kind of horrible monster?
How could I leave my child
my arms are empty
filled by another child
but not really
The child that is here
doesn't replace

the child that is gone
not at all
and I hate myself
for that too
I should enjoy my girl
right there across the room
that tiny smiling face
that reminds me of you
How does a mother choose
between her two children?
Either choice is wrong
either way I loose
This house feels unfinished without you
beautiful old house
full of new dreams
but I don't know how to dream
without you in it
I can't leave you behind
I can't go through the day
I can't forget
Everything reminds me of you
things that I see
things that I do
Even my own face
so like your face
my own heart
an echo of your heartbeat
How can I be without you
How can I go on
build a new life
without you a part of it
I need you here

I need you now
my heart is breaking
That much is clear
How does a mother let a child go?
It feels like death inside me
just so much pain
brokenhearted
when I should be trying
to start up again
I know we all make choices
and we chose this
both of us
eyes wide open
we chose our different paths
but I want you in mine
I want you here now
jealous of the time
you spend with your new someone
Am I deranged?
Children have to leave the nest.
But in this case
the nest was torn from you
sure
I got you a new house but
is that actually enough?
is it a good start for you
out there in the world
So. Fucking. Far. Away.
That is all I can think of
how far away you are
and intellectually I know
I just texted you

this morning
you are only
a phone call away
but it isn't enough
I long for you
child of my heart
and nothing can ever
fill the space that is left
Nothing is enough
to heal this heartbreak

Life is More About the Journey than the Destination

Photo by Jon Flobrant[1] on Unsplash[2]

Walking through the woods
in the quiet and the stillness
of nature
Looking for a path to lead
somewhere exciting and new
enjoying this walk
enjoying the winding trail

1. https://unsplash.com/@jonflobrant?utm_source=medium&utm_medium=referral
2. https://unsplash.com?utm_source=medium&utm_medium=referral

the feel of the wind
through the trees
a feeling of expectation
Not knowing what is around
the next bend
not knowing where I go
And that is ok
we don't always know
where we are going
we don't have to have
all the answers already
We just need to ask
ourselves the right questions
Who am I?
What do I want to be?
What makes me come alive?
What makes me feel free?
The taste of a cup of coffee
the earth beneath my feet
my hands as I write
my heart as I build my dreams
Dreams of rainbows and wishes
for a place to call home
somewhere I feel free
unfettered by worry
a place I can dream
and have dreams feel safe
Visions of somewhere
near or far away
somewhere I can stay
to write these little lines
Somewhere, anywhere

Life goes and flows
we know not where or why
we have taken this path
only we woke up here
as if from a dream
Life is like a dream
like a dance
like a stream
flowing always onward
heading home to the ocean
from the heart of the mountain
And we follow where it leads
Not asking questions
not always wondering why
just following
knowing that we will get
to somewhere someday
but now we are here
now we are safe
now we are free
Do we allow
do we trust
the universe
to guide our way
to find us answers
to unaskable questions
Yes, a voice whispers
yes, trust your heart
trust your inner wisdom
trust the path you are on
The path has twists and turns
and you never know

what you will see next
a waterfall
a butterfly
a forest glade
the shore of the ocean
the bank of a stream
Life takes us ever forward
twisting and turning
like the steps of some
intricate dance
some lost art form
of loving the land
loving the place we are in
no matter the place
Trust in life
trust in yourself
trust in nature
and in the universe
to show us beauty
along the path we walk
in the forest this day

Life of the Unexpected

Sometimes we don't know where the road will take us

Photo by Stan Versluis[1] on Unsplash[2]

Strange places
strange faces
strange roads
turns not taken

1. https://unsplash.com/@stanversluis?utm_source=medium&utm_medium=referral
2. https://unsplash.com?utm_source=medium&utm_medium=referral

How do we know
where the road goes
circling forward
circling back
we find our place
in this new space
learning new things
running this race
Then we stop and sit
for a while by the river
staring at its blue
the green of the trees
feeling the quiet
of the still air
Sometimes in life
we take for granted
everything we have
not realizing
that others have nothing
what we have is so good
yet we squander it
squander our time
spent in restless pursuits
Watching TV again
for another night
all these shows that we
already watched before
not interacting with each other
just passive
how do we learn
to do something more
outside and active

Our souls do crave more
but we fill them with trash
instead of things like love
things with meaning
how do we know
where that meaning is hiding
how do we make the most
of this life we are given?
More peace
more love
more kindness
more fulfillment
more dreams
A wind through the trees
the wings of a bird
things do break the stillness
and we need to take time
to appreciate them

Looking for Me

Photo by Caroline Veronez[1] on Unsplash[2]

Looking for myself
amidst the clutter
inside my mind
Wondering how much is me
how much is the voices
of other people
Their words

1. https://unsplash.com/@carolineveronez?utm_source=medium&utm_medium=referral
2. https://unsplash.com?utm_source=medium&utm_medium=referral

reverberating through my brain
They talk about love languages
they talk about loving
yourself first
before you love other people
but we learn how
to love others first
when we are young
and the form
the opinions that we have
of ourselves
So where do I begin
where do they
leave off?
What is the answer
to these questions
unspoken inside
What do I need to do?
Who am I?
What do I need to be?
How do I love myself?
Do they love me?
So many questions
and no easy answers
to this life I find
and I just question
try to seek the silence
and find peace
find myself waiting
Reaching out to touch
my face in the mirror
see a little clearer

what comes next
what is the chapter
still unwritten
what will fill the pages?
Where am I going?
What am I looking for?
What do I need?
What needs are still unmet?
All these questions
so many questions
so much asking and asking
into the silence of the night
and I look at the moon
in the stillness and wonder
at the meaning of life
I wonder how I fit
into some greater scheme
What is my meaning?
What is my purpose?
Why am I here?
Why do I exist?
Existential questions
looking always upward
always inward
and wondering what
I am supposed to do
to help others
to make the world better
to show love
to those in need
What gift do I have to give?
What do I have to offer?

How can I make a difference?
I look up at the sky
I look into my heart
trying to see more clearly
to find who I am and
how I fit
into this great tapestry
of all life
I want to make a difference
I want to fly
I want to shine
like the stars above
giving my love
giving my heart
my soul
my life
for some greater cause
than just myself
I want to do something
that matters to the world
or just to a girl
my children
I want to leave a legacy
a memory of light
What do we do as souls
casting our gaze
into the night?

Love Can Make You Stronger

Photo by Caleb Ekeroth[1] on Unsplash[2]
Love can make you stronger

or it can bring you to your knees
you never know
what path it will take
or if being held
in your lover's arms
will shut out everything
outside in the world
and keep you safe
love is bright and beautiful
or scarring at your depths
and when we know love
for a long time
it becomes both
love caves in your being
it makes a space inside you
where you carry that person
inside your heart forever
love can take you to heights
or bring you to lows
you thought impossible
and you keep loving on
keep fighting for your love
for the people in your life
who matter more than anything
hold your loved ones close
or let them roam free
as they need this of you
Love should be like wings
that allows you to fly higher
but sometimes

---

1. https://unsplash.com/@calebekeroth?utm_source=medium&utm_medium=referral

2. https://unsplash.com?utm_source=medium&utm_medium=referral

love is more like a chain
pulling your feet down
back to the ground
and it is finding balance
finding the right kind of love
a love that makes you more
makes you grow
that makes you stronger
that is what love is supposed to be
Yet sometimes love falls short
you don't love enough or
they don't love enough or
one of you loves
in a selfish way
and it smothers you
There has to be a balance
between freedom and togetherness
that is the dance that love takes
Love can be a shelter in the storm
or love itself can be the storm
It is for you to decide
to love more brightly
to love more freely
to love with giving
of everything in yourself
a love that makes you more
instead of less
a love that adds joy
and peace to your life
a love built on friendship
and mutual respect
is what we all crave

yet so often
we content ourselves
with a love that is less
We need to learn to love better
in a more whole and healing way
to love so that the person you love
feels like you give them wings

Love Moves in Stillness

Photo by Tyler Nix[1] on Unsplash[2]

1. https://unsplash.com/@nixcreative?utm_source=medium&utm_medium=referral

When we truly love someone
we allow space for them to grow
we allow space for them to be
who they are meant to be
we help them reach for their dreams
and open ourselves for those dreams
we open ourselves up to love
Love is about creating openness
it is about creating trust
it is about creating a refuge
for the other person to call home
You are the one that I love
you are my true north
you are my home
you are the one I come back to
when I go out into the unknown
I always thought you were the wanderer
and I was the place that you came home to
but now it is you that is creating our home
and a place for me to always come back to
Our roles are reversed for the first time
or the last time, or maybe it was always
that both of us made this home together
and it is our love that makes this a home
I am open to your love
I am open to your heart
I am open to hearing your voice
I am open to living your dreams
your dreams are my dreams
and my dreams are your dreams
our live is about being together

---

2. https://unsplash.com?utm_source=medium&utm_medium=referral

and making this a home
Sometimes our love is stillness
sometimes love is movement
love is openness and honesty
and feeling free to be yourself
and you make me always more
of who I am meant to be and
I don't know who I would be
without you, I would be less
Because you help me see
the best in myself always
I hope that I could help you be
the best in yourself too
I hope that I can help you
find the place of your heart
find the place of your dreams
I want to help you and inspire you
and be the place you come home to
when you go out into the world
I want us to build something together
I want to build the world of our dreams
together

Making Hard Choices

How do we know what we are supposed to do?

Photo by Victoriano Izquierdo[1] on Unsplash[2]

How do I know
what path I am supposed to take
uphill or downhill
to the river or the lake?
Where do we go in life

1. https://unsplash.com/@victoriano?utm_source=medium&utm_medium=referral

2. https://unsplash.com?utm_source=medium&utm_medium=referral

always in circles
going somewhere but
we know not where
all the best laid plans
sometimes go astray
And it can be those straying's
that take us the best places
new sights and sounds
strange, new faces
How do we go forward
when do we go back
how do we know
what is supposed to motivate
when we feel lost inside
and found at once
What is the meaning of life
I have asked for years
trying to create method
out of the chaos
But sometimes chaos
is like a beautiful
swirling vortex
taking us to another world
a world full of dreams
Finding love
finding life
finding peace
What is really important
is life just like
the wind through the trees?
following a direction
all its own

pushed by outside forces
Are you rooted like a tree
or free like the wind
or somewhere inbetween
like the flow of a stream
constrained in place
ever moving
How do we grow
how do we know
what is the meaning
what is the day
what are the things
our heart forgets to say?

My Broken Heart

Photo by Marah Bashir[1] on Unsplash[2]

My heart is broken
by choices I have made
that take me far away
from half of my heart
my child
so far away

1. https://unsplash.com/@marahbashir?utm_source=medium&utm_medium=referral

2. https://unsplash.com?utm_source=medium&utm_medium=referral

I don't know what to do
I don't know what to say
don't know what
I could have changed
How do you get someone
to love you most of all
to see your sacrifices
made in silence
all these years
still crying
silent lonely tears
My face is red and swollen
all this crying this morning
I wish I was there with you
I wish...
that so many things were different
that our family wasn't broken
wish I could have grown up
with people who really loved me
the way they love you
I left our family
and don't think you see
that I was drowning there
that I was dying slowly
from their abuse
I know you don't see the scars
formed on my heart
you are young yet
and don't understand
the depths of pain
and suffering for years
I wish you knew...

But then I don't.
no one should know
what it is like to suffer
as much as I have suffered
no one should understand
the depths of this pain
the cuts and the scars
deep down in my heart
No one should feel this
I shielded you
as best I could
from all of the abuse
from all of the hate
from all of the pain
the shame, the blame, the hurt
No, I don't want you to feel this
I don't want you to know what it's like
don't want you to suffer
as I have suffered
I want you to live in sunlight
my innocent golden child
I want you to have your moment
want you to have your love
want you to be filled with joy
And my pain sucks joy away
So far away now from you
from your half of my heart
you are my heart
my first love, my first joy
my first child
half of my heart
will always be yours

Obstacles and Opportunities

Photo by Hu Chen[1] on Unsplash[2]

Do you see the obstacle
or the opportunity
contained within?
Do you see an opportunity
for growth on the hard days
or do you just fall backwards
onto your behind

1. https://unsplash.com/@huchenme?utm_source=medium&utm_medium=referral

2. https://unsplash.com?utm_source=medium&utm_medium=referral

or forwards
onto your face?
Whatever you decide
to see
is what you decide
for yourself to be
You become your thoughts
because all your action
starts in your mind
it is simple
Law of Attraction stuff
for those that know
or kinestethic energy
for those that don't
Simple science
before you do it
you have to dream it
before you become it
you have to see it
Everything starts
out as an idea
Every great achievement
had to be thought up first
before it could be done
And every great accomplishment
had to come first as an opportunity
knocking at someone's door
Will it be your door?
what will you do when
opportunity knocks?
will you open it?
will you let it in?

will you embrace it
with all of your being?
Sometimes we grab opportunity
other times we answer shyly
sometimes we falter
but still we answer the call
we take opportunity
or we just fall
Do you want to take the leap
do you want to make the climb
do you want to dream big
or are you afraid?
I'll tell you a secret my loves
we are all afraid
the dreamers and the doers too
but we are more afraid of
the road not taken
the road that leads to nothing
than we are afraid of the fall
we are afraid if we don't
try something then
we will be nothing at all

On the Edge of Something Great

Photo by Nicholas Sampson[1] on Unsplash[2]

I feel like I am on the edge
lately of something beautiful
of dreams coming true
of hopes coming to light
of all my dreams coming
out of the night
And it feels like something
beautiful is about to happen
like it is finally my time
in so many ways
for my life to blossom
for my life to become whole
and I feel this stirring deep
in the depths of my soul
I feel like my heart
is coming alive
after a long nap
years of hibernation
are coming to an end
and this new spring
has surprises in store
that it will bring
My life is changing
I am changing
I am growing and
expanding my limits
my boundaries growing
wider with this time
taken to heal
and to go within

---

1. https://unsplash.com/@nicholassampson?utm_source=medium&utm_medium=referral

2. https://unsplash.com?utm_source=medium&utm_medium=referral

It is time to come out
like the groundhog
after the long winter
this winter of waiting
to see my shadow is over
and I step into the light
I step out there in front
for all the world to see
looking up at the sky
saying here look at me
I am awake and alive
in this beautiful world
full of opportunity
full of purpose
and I finally know
where my path
is going to go
Forward, onward, upward
Into the light of this new day
that is where I am going
I am coming alive as the world
comes alive again with spring
and everything is beginning
to bud with new life
so has new life
been breathed into me
my spirit renewed
with a sense of peace
and moving forward
at last

Open the Door of the Soul

Photo by Jan Tinneberg[1] on Unsplash[2]

Open the door of the soul
and peer in on what is inside
Find your way inside yourself
to what is hiding there beneath
all of your daily routines
there lies sleeping your soul
there lies the truth of yourself
What is there in the depths

1. https://unsplash.com/@craft_ear?utm_source=medium&utm_medium=referral

2. https://unsplash.com?utm_source=medium&utm_medium=referral

is it clear like a pool
for us to gaze into?
a vast blue water
somewhere inside a cave
beckoning us to dive in
to experience our true selves
our true nature
Return to the Self
return to your soul
return to what hides
down there inside you
In the pool is love
and refreshment
and pure, perfect peace
What lies waiting for you
when you experience yourself?
What lies there inside
always waiting for you
to truly know yourself
to truly be yourself
to free yourself
of all of these things
that seem to chain you
All those things are outside you
and your experience within you
You can know yourself
no matter what is outside
you can see yourself
no matter the turmoil
on the surface of your life
You can find yourself
always there waiting

deep inside your heart
that pool of stillness
that place of deep waters
that lies in wait for you
You can find your true north
if you look at your inner compass
You can be yourself
you can live in freedom
from what you experience
if you go inside yourself
YOU are always hiding there
just lying in wait for yourself
the true essence of the Self
the boundless nature of being
Find yourself again
find yourself,
it is freeing

Pulled in Two Directions

Sometimes it hurts being pulled from too many directions

Photo by KARTIK GADA[1] on Unsplash[2]

Where am I being pulled
towards or away
either way is away
from somewhere I want to go
and it kills me inside
So I am stuck here
directionless
floundering
wondering
if I made the wrong choice
Two lives
you only get to choose
one
And I don't know
if I made the right choice
being pulled back
like a rubber band
about to snap
Tears fall down now
with regret
for what I didn't have
the life I didn't choose
wondering
if I chose wrong
Up all night
sleep all day
if you count sleeping
as lying in bed crying

---

1. https://unsplash.com/@kartikgada?utm_source=medium&utm_medium=referral

2. https://unsplash.com?utm_source=medium&utm_medium=referral

Sands of Time

Photo by Aron Visuals[1] on Unsplash[2]

We are all grains of sand
in the hourglass of time
passing forth slowly
through this vast expanse
of the great universe
We are just a grain of sand
on a beach
with other grains of sand

1. https://unsplash.com/@aronvisuals?utm_source=medium&utm_medium=referral
2. https://unsplash.com?utm_source=medium&utm_medium=referral

chipped from great rocks
by the motion of the sea
We linger here
pieces of something bigger
something greater
than ourselves
We see ourselves
as the center of the universe
but really the universe is vast
and we are just so small
If you look at the fabric
of the night sky
our world is just
a tiny speck
in this vast field of darkness
and even our bright sun
just another tiny star
when seen from far away
We think ourselves large
our lives are just about us
but we are part of something
greater than our own experience
we are the sum of all time
flowing past in the universe
we are the culmination
of years and years
of work on this earth
years of discovery
evolution of technology
evolution of thought
We are just small
pieces and fragments

of something greater
and when we see that
we can take ourselves
and our lives less seriously
We can know that we are part
of this vast whole
of something so much greater
than we ourselves could dream
or even begin to fathom

Searching for Meaning

Photo by Daniel Lerman[1] on Unsplash[2]

Much of life
is a search for meaning
to find what matters
inside the madness
We find ourselves
find our souls
find love
find a sense of purpose

1. https://unsplash.com/@dlerman6?utm_source=medium&utm_medium=referral
2. https://unsplash.com?utm_source=medium&utm_medium=referral

find words in the silence
that speak to our hearts
It feels like always
we are seeking something more
wandering onward
to a distant shore
What is it that drives us
that pushes us on
what helps us stay strong
and stay on the path
Where do we go
when there is no path?
Flowing like a rushing stream
or dripping like the rain
always going somewhere
always going on
What is it that makes us
want this forward motion
instead of staying still
it feels like staying stuck
to be stagnant
unmoving
unyielding
But trees stay still
and they grow
should we be rooted
like a tree
instead of flowing
like the water
What are we supposed to be?
Silence or speech?
stillness or motion?

Is there a right or a wrong answer?
I wonder
what is the meaning
of life that we find
in the small moments
and the big dreams
what is it that
makes us feel alive
that keeps us going
through the dark times?

Seeing Yourself Again

Photo by Pixabay

Reflection of my face
there in the mirror
but what do I see
what is hiding
there in my eyes?
What realizations
hide behind
my placid face?
It feels like seeing
only half the picture

not what lies within
behind my eyes
the window to the soul
what is reflected there
what knowledge
what peace?
I don't know
all the answers yet
or even the questions
I am supposed to ask
like a child again
on this spiritual path
beginning again
from somewhere new
what can I be
am I someone who
can achieve realization
enlightenment
nirvana
Can I find the answers
that I seek
to life and myself
to all that is?
I ponder the meaning
of life again
It has been a long time
I have been so far
but come back
in a circle
to where I used to be
and I don't know
where I am going

this time
I am going slower
more intentional
and I want to know
where do I go
from here?
Go inward
behind those eyes
seek the silence
and the stillness
of the mind
what answers
are there to find?
I want to know it all
see it all
be it all
but is that possible?
I want to dissolve
into the endless now
the heart of the universe
I want to merge
with all that is
to find the answers
out there in the stars
the silence of the night
falling from the sky
shooting star
I want to find
what lies behind
all those mysteries
of the universe
all the sands of time

I want to be like a drop
of rain falling
from the sky above
into the ocean
our mother
the waves crashing endlessly
against every shore
following the moon
in the silence of the night
I want it to be right
this time
How do you find
which answer is right?
Is there just one answer
or many like the stars?
Does each soul
have an answer
all its own?
Do we all know
just a piece of wisdom
instead of being able
to know it all
to see it all
or do we just see
a small piece
of eternity?

Seeking for the Truth

LAO TSU:

"THOSE WHO KNOW DO NOT SPEAK. THOSE WHO SPEAK DO NOT KNOW."

WWW.MILLENIALMOM.NET

Photo created with canva.

"Those who know do not speak. Those who speak do not know."

— Lao Tsu, Tao Teh Ching[1]

What is life but a journey

---

1. https://www.goodreads.com/work/quotes/100074

Seeking for ourselves
seeking for our truth
the great truth of all things
that lies sleeping within us
How do we find ourselves?
we were here all the time
quietly waiting
to be found
How do we heal our hearts
from the scars of time
but with love
that is already within us
Love is our true nature
love is ourselves
our lives
our being
but we forget
We try to fill up
the empty space within
instead of realizing
we are meant to be empty
we are meant to be at peace
How do we find ourselves
when we were never lost
how do we come full circle
to see that where we are
is where we were always meant to be

Shallow Grave

Photo by Denny Müller[1] on Unsplash[2]

I feel like I have been buried
in this shallow grave
only half alive
half dead
Maybe more dead
is what they thought me
to bury me still alive
Or though I yet breathe

1. https://unsplash.com/@redaquamedia?utm_source=medium&utm_medium=referral

2. https://unsplash.com?utm_source=medium&utm_medium=referral

maybe life has gone from me
Leaving behind all the things
that were supposed to mean something
leaving behind my life
and finding nothing in return
only emptiness inside
where my heart used to be
You see I cut it out
and locked it away
afraid of getting hurt
again another day
Hurt so much before
yet longing for something else
something more
But not finding what I longed for
I cut out my useless heart
and threw it away
so here I lie now
in this shallow grave
in a field of the dead
shrouded in mist and stillness
it is here that I awake
I claw at the lid of the coffin
in which I am sealed
looking for air
or a way out
pushing, pulling
and digging through
the soft earth entombing me
in this fresh grave
not yet hardened ground
I claw my way out

bleeding fingers
and realize I should
go looking for my heart
become alive again
with its beating
Try again to live
try again to love
Though love may be fleeting
it can be worth the pain
it is less painful
then being buried alive

Shrouded in Midnight

Photo by Riccardo Mion[1] on Unsplash[2]

She sits in the darkness
waiting for her lost love
looking at the stars
and the moon up above
Long ago she loved him
long ago she lost
yet still the feelings
linger on

1. https://unsplash.com/@riccardomion?utm_source=medium&utm_medium=referral

2. https://unsplash.com?utm_source=medium&utm_medium=referral

reminding her
of the touch of his fingers
on her gentle skin
She used to be a young girl then
now she is a woman
a thing of the world
not so innocent
but still not yet wise
or she would stop
this pining
He isn't coming here
to this clearing to meet her
just the moon
is her lover tonight
just the sky
as she dances
under the night
The witching hour
they call it
and she doesn't disappoint
for she and her sisters
call to the night
their dark power
far from the light
She whirls faster
and faster now
a curse she wants to bring
to that man who hurt her
that lover
of long ago
who left scars
on her heart

and on her skin
She remembers
the way he broke
her heart
and her bones
she remembers clearly
the place they called home
yet no longer
she has a new home
she is stronger now
braver
she has learned to say no
and say it loudly
But now she says
something else entirely
dark words
to bring dark magic

Spirit Speaks in Silence

Photo by Yannic Läderach[1] on Unsplash[2]

For many years we have walked
asleep
forgetting ourselves and
our true nature of peace

1. https://unsplash.com/@yl_photography?utm_source=medium&utm_medium=referral

2. https://unsplash.com?utm_source=medium&utm_medium=referral

our inner love and light
hidden under a barrel
of our own making
Broken and bruised hands
keep writing on
trying to find hope
find love
find the light again
in the darkness of the night
trying to find aliveness
in the dead of winter
Yet somewhere underneath
the snow covered ground
lie seeds, asleep
waiting to grow when the ground thaws
Our lives are like that
waiting for the freeze to lift
so that we can grow
and connect to the light
of spirit once again
How do we find ourselves
we go within
we seek the silence
we find inner peace
inner wisdom
the truth of our hearts
for we know
we all know the answers
Love more.
Be more kind.
Trust more.
Show compassion always.

Other than that,
there is no answer
the answer is love
which is the light of our being
love that comes from within
and shines outward
to the rest of the world
My lovelies,
uncover your light
let yourself shine
set your brightness free
let your heart be untamed
your soul at peace
How you ask me?
Stay still.
just breathe.
become one with your breath
one with yourself
safe in the stillness
and peace of your heart
Remember who you are
come awake
come alive
become aware
of everything flowing through you
your life force
is the life force of all
and it is with you always
this boundless love
this boundless light
it is who you are
your true nature

your true self
and it is boundless
Fly on the wings of your heart
go towards the land of your dreams
find yourself free again
in the open sky
allow yourself to fly
allow yourself to surrender
to remember
to be all that you are
Love, light, peace
eternity
a piece of life's heart

Still Searching

Photo by Warren Wong[1] on Unsplash[2]
Still searching for myself
still searching for some truth
some answer to these questions
that I feel myself asking
into the dead of the night
the silence of the early morning
and none of the answers feel right
just bring more questions
like I have gone into the depths of the ocean
to find a sunken treasure and
found only a space
where something used to be buried
found by someone else
and now
there is just a hole
where the treasure used to be
I got there too late
got to the place I was looking for only
to find the place had been moved
like the tombs of the pharos
looted long ago
in some time unremembered
something that used to be beautiful
now it is just empty and hollow
a shell of what used to be there
Like walking a ruined city and wondering
at the lives of the people that lived there
long ago
in a time forgotten

---

1. https://unsplash.com/@wflwong?utm_source=medium&utm_medium=referral

2. https://unsplash.com?utm_source=medium&utm_medium=referral

and wondering
why those people left
where did they go?
Is it the aftermath of Vesuvius?
Or more like Croatoan?
Is there some natural phenomenon
that spurred the people from the empty streets
or is it just an unanswerable question
that no one knows
did they go somewhere?
or, did they just disappear?
I feel like I have disappeared too
from the face of reality
from the face of a normal life
I live in a space of limbo
like staring back at my own life from outer space
so far away from everything
What is my life supposed to be?
what am I supposed to be doing?
where am I supposed to be going?
All I have is questions
like clawing skeleton hands
tearing at my soft flesh
and I bleed slowly
silently scream into the darkness
longing to be free of this pain
this questioning
this unsureness
I wish that answers were simple
but the answers to the deep questions
seldom are

Swollen Eyes

Photo by Chaozzy Lin[1] on Unsplash[2]

Eyes swollen
from too much crying
so much hurt
so many years
I felt so alone
cried so many tears
always alone
I never wanted

1. https://unsplash.com/@chaozzy?utm_source=medium&utm_medium=referral

2. https://unsplash.com?utm_source=medium&utm_medium=referral

to cry
in front of people
People take crying
too seriously
they don't understand
sometimes you need
to let the feelings out
so they aren't trapped
inside melting you
tearing you apart
from the inside
Tears are the feelings
going away
relief, pain, fear, sadness
so many reasons to cry
yet so often
we are asked to deny
our own feelings
to push them down
hurting so much
it can make you drown
Yet still sometimes
I wish
someone would
hold me while I cry
so I wasn't so alone
so the pain could be shared
rather than to just
be a burden to someone else
I am tired of always
being a burden
to someone

I want my feelings
to be alright
I want to be able
to cry without a fight
Sometimes I just want
to feel less alone
though I am in
a crowded room
yet it is a room where
I can't make my feelings
ever known
People don't want
your truth
people just want
things to be easier
they just want
what is surface-level
The softer side of me
the side
you didn't want to see
If you believed I was hard
it would be easier
for you to be unkind
but when you see the tears
you know I am less
than being happy
I am not perfect either
I am just like you
I know you cry too
or you should
with everything
you have been through

How do we move forward?
How do we move past?
How do we build something
that can really last?
It is always the ones
we love most who hurt us
because they are the ones
with our lives
in their hands
strangers don't have that
they don't have the power
It is friends, family, lovers
they control our feelings
they feed our thoughts
hold our hearts
in their hands
How do we know
if we are going to be
the cause of pain
for someone else?
How do we know if
we can help them
feel a bit better
lend a helping hand
pull them up
from where they are lying
and we need help
all of us
We need loved ones
to share our lives with
we need friends, lovers, family
to enrich our lives

Yet still
we have to be strong
move forward
let the feelings
pass along
My eyes are swollen
from a night of crying
but today they are dry
filled with some hope
some perspective
some ideas
on how to be differently
for the next time
a power struggle erupts

The Box in the Corner

image by Mario Hofer[1] from Pixabay[2]

Sometimes there are pieces
of yourself
you try to erase
but you end up realizing

1. https://pixabay.com/de/users/homar-318270/?utm_source=link-attribution&utm_medium=referral&utm_campaign=image&utm_content=1935027
2. https://pixabay.com/de/?utm_source=link-attribution&utm_medium=referral&utm_campaign=image&utm_content=1935027

that all you can do is
stuff them down
put them away
Sometimes far away
like a locked chest
in the corner
of some forgotten room
First you put it there
you forget about it
then years pass
and you stack
other things
on top of it
but it's still there
underneath
still waiting
to be uncovered
And then you find
yourself longing
for those things
dark things
locked within
Your forgotten fears
mingled with your
ancient wisdom
all those dark nights
of your soul
where you suffered
you locked away
before you found
a balm for your pain
Still you can feel it

calling to you
beckoning you backward
to unlock the chest
the parts of yourself
left long untouched
long to feel
the caress of fingertips
Longing like a lover
beckoning you back
for a night
of loving again
Do you regret
those things you locked away
so long ago
do they call to you
beckoning you backward
come home my love
come home they say
come be yourself
come have your day
Come back and find us
your loneliness
your loss
your pain
your wisdom
your beauty
your glory
For when you lock up feelings
you don't realize that
it's the good with the bad
or, the things you deemed
bad anyway

You can't cut off a piece of yourself
just lock it up in that box
and forget where you laid
the key
But eventually
after searching and seeking
you find the rusted key
and put it to the lock
looking for what
hides inside
Your longing
which begets your love
your pain
which shows your healing
your scars
which show your strength
your anger
which shows your boundaries
All these things
that you locked away
have a deeper meaning
a deeper purpose
than just to hurt you
for it is through our hurt
that we learn to be whole
It is through our wanting
that our wants
can be realized
And it is through our searching
that answers are found
Trying to live without them
we live only half alive

a shell of a person
without feelings inside
Two sides
of the same coin are we
our darkness and light
are comingled within us
bringing us higher
levels of realization
but only together
only when we learn unity
that we must create all
the shades of gray in between
the dark and the light
that is where colors blossom
in the inbetween times
not at either extreme
we need both
in order to be anything
and sometimes we forget
we make ourselves less
thinking we make ourselves safe
Safe, sure
but what is that?
it is the absence of fear
but also the absence of joy
it is the absence of tears
and the absence of laughter
We have to learn this
sometimes the hard way
for those of us
who are stubborn
Being a seeker is hard

and sometimes we don't want
to seek anymore
but we can't quite get rid
of those things in that box
it is a part of us
no matter how small
waiting there always
waiting to be opened

The Holes Life Caves into Our Being

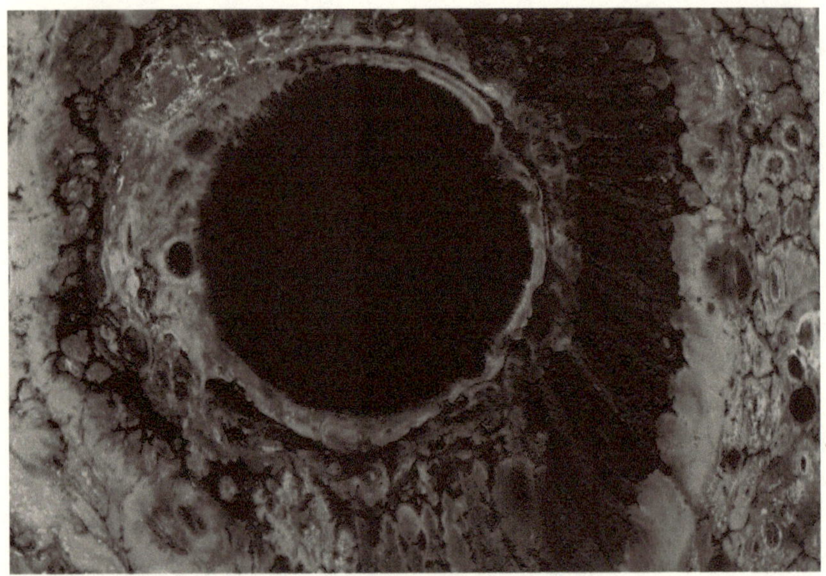

Photo by Pawel Czerwinski[1] on Unsplash[2]

As we go through life
pain carves holes into our being
like places where love
Once lived then flowed out
It is only the things
that we have loved
that can hurt us
Only the times we have held on

1. https://unsplash.com/@pawel_czerwinski?utm_source=medium&utm_medium=referral

2. https://unsplash.com?utm_source=medium&utm_medium=referral

that can make us let go
sometimes violently
Sadness carves holes in our hearts
letting everything fall away
leaving only silence
only emptiness
in the wake of the pathways of tears
that once fell
Feeling nothing is worse than
feeling sad
the angry emptiness
where something used to be
Like the empty space on the shelf
where the broken cup
used to stand
The empty holes in our hearts
are like that
a monument
to emptiness
a place where things broke
a place where things fell out
Emptiness and apathy
the worst part of depression
Worse than the pain
worse than the anger
worse than the sadness
Like the eye of the storm
when you know that worse
is yet to come
Time waits
and we feel these heartbeats
in the stillness

of the night
just waiting
for what the light of day brings
Something bright and beautiful?
Or more sadness, anger and pain?

The Journey of Life

Photo by Johannes Plenio[1] on Unsplash[2]

We walk our path
on this journey of life
going a little forward
through the trees
and we feel lost sometimes
in these great woods
this forest of the world
We want to go home
but know not where
home is found
Finding new homes

1. https://unsplash.com/@jplenio?utm_source=medium&utm_medium=referral
2. https://unsplash.com?utm_source=medium&utm_medium=referral

along our way
finding a place
where perhaps we can stay
Other people on our path
walk with us for a time
giving us love
friendship and shelter
Walking together
on this journey home
to the place we came from
so long ago
We know not where
the journey begins or ends
we start in the middle somewhere
and go in this vast circle
leading us back home
to where we came from
in time unremembered
Sometimes we stumble
or take a different path
lose our companions
or go to scout ahead
sometimes loved
sometimes lonely
but we know
we will find each other again
as we circle ever closer
In this vast, wide world
there is much to be learned
much wisdom and heartache
comingled together
We look for our way

we look for a light
we look for each other
trying to hold on
and keep things together
It is better to walk together
or so we often think
yet sometimes
there are paths
we must take alone
for it is longing
that is the birthplace of love

The Journey On

Photo by Harsh Gupta[1] on Unsplash[2]

The Chinese philosopher Lao Tzu said; "**The journey of a thousand miles begins with one step**"

Sometimes one step forward
is all we can take
sometimes a smile or a laugh
feels forced and fake
When you feel sad
keep going
when you feel lost
look for a guide
to show you the way
a map
a light at the end of the tunnel
a sign
to keep you moving forward
Even if you have to stop
and rest a while
that's ok
we all need rest
we all need strength
to return to wholeness
We can't see the whole picture
just a piece
of the vast puzzle
that is life
Find strength for one more step
even if you stumble
Look for one more piece
to put into the puzzle
One more day

---

1. https://unsplash.com/@imharsh081?utm_source=medium&utm_medium=referral
2. https://unsplash.com?utm_source=medium&utm_medium=referral

one more hope
to overcome your fear
keep going
even when you stumble
keep speaking
even when you mumble
Who knows
the words you say
may be what someone else needs too
The words you need for yourself
can help to inspire others
Just one step
can be enough for today
just one word
on a blank page
just one smile
at yourself in the mirror
Sometimes small is all we have
sometimes frightened is
our state of being
but fear gives us space
for bravery
that's what it is
to keep going when you fear
you are brave
you haven't given up
though you falter
you do not stop
though you are sad
you don't let the tears
overcome and control you
Stop listening to the voices

always telling you no
and say yes
to yourself instead
say yes to keeping going
say yes to today
say yes to love
say yes to hope
say yes to embracing change
say yes to forgiveness
even if you say it to yourself
only half believing
the words you say to yourself
are the biggest strength you have
and you get to choose them
You get to choose what to be
no matter how you feel
you choose yourself
you choose the people
with you in your life
you choose to keep going
in spite of it all
sometimes one step
no matter how small
is all you have in you
and that's ok
Take that one step
speak that one word
Keep going on
even if you start small
because sometimes small
is all you have inside
but small is enough

it is the single candle flame
to light the darkness
it is the single dream of love
and of the future
of yourself
to sustain yourself
for one more breath
Take that one breath
focus on your heart
you are still alive
and that is always enough

The Joys and Sorrows of Motherhood

Watching your kids go their own way

Photo owned by Author

My heart lives with yours
It beats with you
stays with you
in the darkness
of this night
far away though you are
I love you with everything
child of my heart
child of my soul

I gave you everything
I gave you all
that was within my reach
But now you are out of reach
now you have grown and
have to find your own way
I hope you find your truth
a path of love and beauty
the dreams of your soul
made manifest in the world
I hope that your struggles
are soon overcome
though I know in life
there will be more
but they can consume you
or make you stronger
as you learn to be more
than the things that hurt you
Shadows in the night
like clawing hands
obscuring the light
nightmares instead of dreams
I know you see this night
Know that you are not alone
you have hands to hold
a voice to soothe and calm
mother, friends, lover
to calm your nerves
we are here for you
all of us in a circle
to hold you upright
though you may fall

so many hands to hold you
beautiful girl
so many people to love you
not just mother now
You are married now and have
your own little family
but please know
you are still always
part of mine too
my family and my heart
my dreams
inspiration for my art
inspiration to be
a better mother
a better human
I hope you find people
who inspire you too
to be the best you can be
to give you wings
to fly to your dreams
I hope your struggles ease
I hope you somehow
find a measure of peace
that you find rest
for this night and
tomorrow wake refreshed
with the new light
of a new day
I hope that you grow
into all the things
I know you can be
I hope you believe in yourself

the way I believe in you
know that you are strong
beyond measure
and a match for any
troubles that may find you
Be well, my child
though child you are
no more
out there in the world
know that I am only
a phone call away
Always.

Key Message: As mothers, our hearts always live wherever our children are.

The Light Comes Again

Photo by Rachel Cook[1] on Unsplash[2]

1. https://unsplash.com/@grafixgurl247?utm_source=medium&utm_medium=referral

Every dark night
comes to an end
with the bright light
of the sunrise
The quiet of the morning
bringing stillness
light and peace
A new hope
a new dream
a new chance
to be what you want to be
There is contrast in life
light and darkness
hope and fear
love and pain
and over time
inside you find balance
between different aspects
of yourself and your life
What is it that gives you meaning?
What is it that gives you hope?
What could be more glorious
than the beauty of a new day
a new morning
beckoning you forward
to greet the sun
to greet yourself again
in the light of day
the darkness dispelled
free from your pain
Come forward my loves

---

2. https://unsplash.com?utm_source=medium&utm_medium=referral

into the light of the day
leave your dreams of darkness
come forward and play

The Road Less Traveled

Photo by Eric Muhr[1] on Unsplash[2]

Do you want to take
the main street
where everyone goes?
Or, do you want to
take the road less traveled
into the woods
steep and dark
through the trees

1. https://unsplash.com/@ericmuhr?utm_source=medium&utm_medium=referral

2. https://unsplash.com?utm_source=medium&utm_medium=referral

Do you want to see
what everyone sees?
Or, do you want to see
something new
seen only by
some brave few?
Is it time for average?
Or time to face your fears?
If you go where
everyone goes you
will do what
everyone has done
already
But if you go the forest track
the road less traveled
you will see something rare
something beautiful
or terrifying
but something new
something different
you will be unique
with unique thoughts
and experiences
all your own
Do you want the average life
or the life of the unknown?
do you want to go in the woods
or stay in your comfort zone?
Life is up to you
it depends on your path
it depends on your road
where you go

who you see
what you do
Will you be a cookie cutter
with a Starbucks drink
or will you be
something else?

The Road Life Takes

Photo by Karsten Würth[1] on Unsplash[2]

The road we take
may have twists and turns
and take you in many
different directions
Sometimes the road
is straight and we travel swiftly
sometimes the road
takes turns

1. https://unsplash.com/@karsten_wuerth?utm_source=medium&utm_medium=referral

2. https://unsplash.com?utm_source=medium&utm_medium=referral

and we travel slowly
uphill through the trees
or along the cliffs
of the ocean
crossing rivers
crossing streams
going over rocks
and we don't know
when it will
get easy again
But it does
It does get easier again
the road gets smoother
it gets straighter
We can go faster
through the vast landscape
That is what life is
a road going somewhere
always forward
always onward
going somewhere
and we don't know
when it will end
we don't know
how far we will go
So much time
so much ground to cover
so much life to live
We don't always know
what we will find
around the next bend
Sometimes stumble on

we keep going forward
keep trying
keep striving
trying to find our way
through the darkness
into the light of day

The Road Not Taken

Photo by Jack Skinner[1] on Unsplash[2]

In life there are so many

paths for us to take
some leading here
some leading there
some circling back
to where we began
And I wonder now
with the darkness
of the early morning
about roads not taken
about chances lost
and choices made
Wonder if I did right
or if I left behind
things and people
that should have been
right by my side
So many twists
and turns of the road
and what lies ahead
is often unseen
and we have to guess
at what comes next
So when do we look back
when do we circle
back to where we started
older and wiser now
looking in the mirror
and wondering how
the years went by so fast
Choices made when

---

1. https://unsplash.com/@jack_skinner?utm_source=medium&utm_medium=referral

2. https://unsplash.com?utm_source=medium&utm_medium=referral

we were so much younger
more naïve and hopeful
about the way things
could be in the future
but the future is now
and I stand looking back
at so many forks
in the road behind me
Where did those other paths lead?
This is the question
that I whisper now
as if from a dream
in to the darkness
of this half-formed day
and I ask myself
is what is ahead greater
than what was left behind
There is no way to know that
not now, not ever
our life is chosen and
we can't go back and un-choose
We have to embrace the day
and the choices we have made
and move forward now
get up and face the day
moving always forward
never circling back
except in errant thought
and accept our choices
as they are today
Each day brings new choices
new chances for all things

love, happiness, hope, greatness
There is so much
that lies ahead of us
if we face towards the future
instead of furtively glancing back

The Silence Demands Decisions

Photo by Jeffrey Keenan[1] on Unsplash[2]

Where is this path taking me?
I know I have to decide
and I am stuck
in indecision
I don't like my choices
and I know I need to find
a better third option
The lesser of two evils

1. https://unsplash.com/@jeffreykeenan?utm_source=medium&utm_medium=referral

2. https://unsplash.com?utm_source=medium&utm_medium=referral

is never really a choice
it just means
that the solution
hasn't presented itself
yet
Not yet
wait
be patient
seek the stillness
of your soul
and the answer
that will set you free
from the madness
You always have a choice
a multitude of choices
This way?
That way?
Some other way?
I keep believing
perhaps foolishly
that there is always
some other way
and if I can quiet myself
quiet these feelings
I will find it waiting
for me in the stillness
in the dark recesses
of the back of my mind
Follow your heart
they always say
but what about when your heart
is being pulled

in different directions
by different people?
How do you know
who you love most?
How do you know
who you can't live without?
The real answer is hiding
obscured
through the lens of sadness
shame and regret
at chances lost
roads not taken
and I just wonder
is it too late
to turn back now?
Is it too late
to build something better?
to heal what is broken?
Whispers of the wind
tell me something is coming
some answer unseen
and I need to be open
Open eyes
open mind
open heart
Seek the stillness and find
a new dream hiding there
a new way forward
through the darkness of the trees
leading somewhere
down this dark path
somewhere there is light

somewhere there is peace
there is an answer
there has to be

The World is Full of Beautiful People Today I realized it on TikTok

Photo by Greg Rakozy[1] on Unsplash[2]

The world is full
of people with beautiful souls
people trying with kindness
to help each other grow
Nourishing each other
providing solace
like a warm blanket

1. https://unsplash.com/@grakozy?utm_source=medium&utm_medium=referral
2. https://unsplash.com?utm_source=medium&utm_medium=referral

on this cold October day
People really do care
you can see it in their eyes
in their actions
in their smiles
There are so many good people
in this bright world of ours
it is just up to us to find them
and be inspired by them
then
to become them
and inspire someone else
We can all light
a match to a flame
and light up the world
Move away from blame
to hope again
There is always hope
in the darkest days
and there is always light
in the darkest night
even if it is just
a faint faraway star
if we move closer
that star is a beautiful sun
shining for some otherworld
The world is beautiful
full of good people
full of hopes and dreams
full of goodness and love
full of light
We just have to turn sometimes

to see it
sometimes our shadow tells us
we are facing
away from the light and
its time to turn around
and face the sun

Things I Said When I was Depressed

Photo by Mitchell Hartley[1] on Unsplash[2]

There were things I said

when I was depressed
true? untrue?
They were true at the time
But maybe something I otherwise
never would have said
maybe thought
but not dwelled on and
for sure not given voice
Like they say
a drunk man's words
are a sober man's thoughts
But when we are depressed
we believe the worst of our thoughts
Maybe usually we wouldn't
maybe we don't want to
maybe we are lying to ourselves
with forced toxic positivity
trying to turn our feelings around
Thoughts and feelings swirl
beneath the surface of the mind
like a whirlpool
trying to pull the ship down
Sometimes I wonder
if what I think is true
if I can believe my own mind
or if my mind is the enemy
They say mind over matter
but what about when your mind
is what is the matter?
How do you know what to believe

---

1. https://unsplash.com/@mtchllhrtly?utm_source=medium&utm_medium=referral

2. https://unsplash.com?utm_source=medium&utm_medium=referral

when you can't believe yourself?
It is like two halves of you
are at war
the feelings
and the rationality
How do you know what to think
when all your thoughts
feel far away
like you are drowning
in quicksand
and barely keeping your head
where you can breathe
What then?
What do you believe
when you can't believe yourself?
What do you say
when you are drowning
and try to ask for help
Sometimes all you can say is
"I need help"
not what you actually
might need help with
because you don't know
you need help with everything
even the smallest things
like getting out of bed
brushing your teeth
doing the dishes
anything but sleeping
and sometimes even that
How do you get help
when you can't articulate your thoughts?

Me, who always has something to say
isn't it ironic
Sometimes I don't know what to say
just that I need to say something
I am clawing my way up
from the bottom of a well
I am drowning
please throw me a line
please save me
from the darkness of myself
please help me
I don't know how to tell you
how to help me
because in that moment
I don't know
All I know is
I am drowning
I am dying
I am broken
I am bleeding
I am lying on the ground
and I need you to fix it
because I can't
I can't fix it when I feel broken
Sometimes it just takes time
or a trip to the doctor
or the ER
but other times
just getting to the doctor
picking up the phone
getting in the car
seems an insurmountable task

I am drowning
Someone help me
that is all I can say
everything else
coming out of my mouth
is just window dressing
I am begging for help and
If you don't help I am angry
I am livid
I am raging
I am broken
I want to scream in your face
please help me dammit
I don't know what I need
I don't know what you can do
but I am dying
that is all that I know.

Troubled Dreams

Photo by Kinga Cichewicz[1] on Unsplash[2]

This morning I wake
disoriented
from troubled dreams
again last night
and I wonder
how long this will last
Dreams are windows
to our souls and our psyche

1. https://unsplash.com/@all_who_wander?utm_source=medium&utm_medium=referral
2. https://unsplash.com?utm_source=medium&utm_medium=referral

they tell us secrets
in whispers of the night
what are these whispers saying?
I am still not healed
not completely
there are still frayed edges
here and there
and I wonder if
it will always be so
That is what the dreams
seem to whisper
in the silence of the night
they whisper
that I am still afraid
of hands clutching at me
out of the darkness
Can they reach this far?
across the sea
across time
these hands
that clutch at me
in my dreams at night
it seems they can
But what about in the daylight?
does that make the dreams
grow silent?
to leave only this vague
sense of uneasiness
that lingers on
into the daylight again
Another day of unease
another night of dreams

fitful sleep
reaching for peace
reaching for silence
an end to these dreams

Unhealed Wounds

Photo by Hannah Xu[1] on Unsplash[2]

Your unhealed wounds
become more apparent
around the holidays
thinking of things past
and long ago
but still not healed
Like scars from cut marks
they don't go away

1. https://unsplash.com/@ohshoothannah?utm_source=medium&utm_medium=referral
2. https://unsplash.com?utm_source=medium&utm_medium=referral

no matter how far
you may go from home
Christmases past
when you weren't happy
shining or bright
and you wonder how
to move forward now
that things have changed
You have changed too
but how much?
you begin to wonder
and how to move on
how to let go
how to forget
Stop living in the past
and live today
in a different way
happier than before
a new start
in a new place
should provide that
Somehow though still
all the memories come
How do you run
how do you get free?
from the past
and I wonder
what to think
what to do now
How do you forget
everything that came before
how do you accept

now that it is over
that you are safe
from being hurt like that again
you aren't under threat
you are safe and free
Remember that
remember that you are safe
that you are free
that those hands
are in the past
those people are gone
across the ocean
far away
The past is far away
so why does it still
clutch at us this way

We Are Blind

Photo by Ganapathy Kumar[1] on Unsplash[2]

We are blind to love
we are blind to life
we are blind to feelings
circling around
We get so caught up
in this rat race of life
we forget what is important
forget what has meaning
forget all the things

1. https://unsplash.com/@gkumar2175?utm_source=medium&utm_medium=referral

2. https://unsplash.com?utm_source=medium&utm_medium=referral

that made life worth it
in the first place
How do we let ourselves go blind?
We start focusing on money
which is just a means to an end
and forget
that it isn't the end in itself
We let go of our values
and we forget who we are
forget what we are supposed to do
what we really wanted
before all these shiny distractions came
We go blind willfully
poking out our own eyes
as we go astray
go a different way
than our hearts wanted to go
and we forget our true selves
forget our meaning
How do we remember
how do we rekindle
the flames of our hearts
heal our eyes to see again
the dreams of our youth
How do we reclaim our passions
reignite our hopes
we need to come alive again
we need to remember who we are
who we are supposed to be
who we were meant to be
and really want to be
Like the moon on a cloudless night

we can see again
even through the night
we can come alive again
we can find the light

We are Made from Stardust

Photo by Kristopher Roller[1] on Unsplash[2]

We are made of stardust
and something special
a kind of energy
neither created or destroyed
we are particles
of some grand design
and we exist here
stranded in time

1. https://unsplash.com/@krisroller?utm_source=medium&utm_medium=referral

2. https://unsplash.com?utm_source=medium&utm_medium=referral

Life is beautiful and vast
and we are tiny specks
yet we are part
of this vast fabric
of the universe
we are a single stich
in this tapestry
all woven together
in its intricacies
We are like a drop of water
flowing back to the ocean
and our vast mother
crashes endlessly
against every shore
the moon and the tides
moving in rhythm
guiding us onward
We move in this dance
all of us dancers whirling
like a dervish in the sand
and we,
only grains of that sand
We move in stillness
we move with music
the notes in a symphony
and we each
just a single note
in its vast beauty
We are small as grains
or stardust flying
through the vastness of space
specks of dust

on this blue planet
made up of more stardust
How do we know our place?
are we already there?
grains of sand in the hourglass
of all time
and we are just here
for this small moment
in the millennia
We are all so small
but together
we are more
we are the fabric
of all that is and was
and is to come
Stronger together
we build something
that can outlast time itself
because we are time
we are movement
we are life
All like cells
in the body of the universe
pieces of her beating heart
and we give her life
give her breath
we are the life force
of the universe
vibrating softly
there in that great body
We are stardust
yet in our oneness

we are the sky and the stars
all in one
As we come together
we become more
than tiny grains of sand
or drops of water
or stitches in a fabric
We become a vast oneness
we become everything

What Makes You Feel Alive?

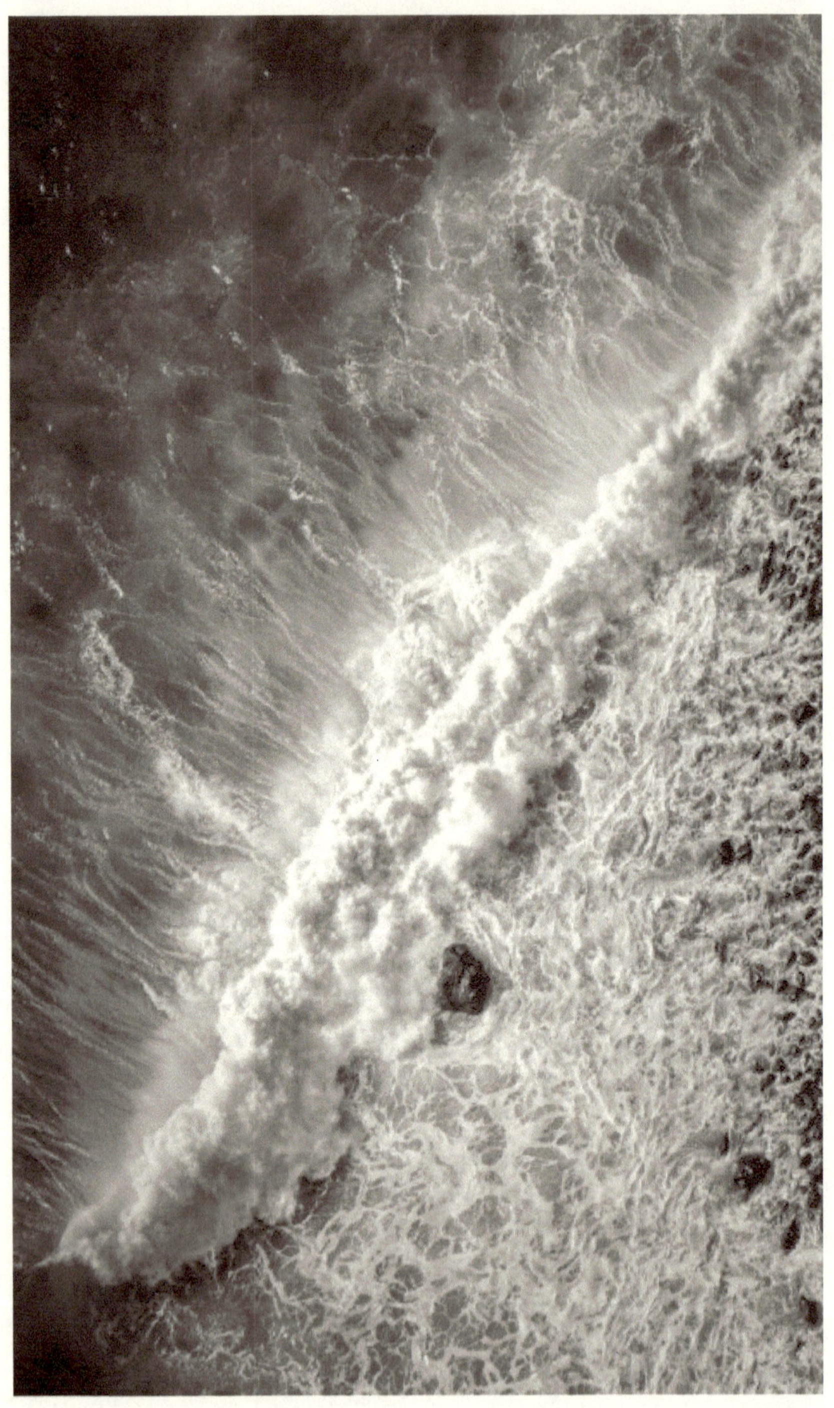

Photo by Gatis Marcinkevics[1] on Unsplash[2]
Nothing makes me feel alive
like standing beside the ocean
staring quietly
into the night
There is this beauty and power
in the waves as they crash
Going this way
going that
finding the shore
day after day
time after time
in rhythm
with the movements of life
with the moon
with the tide
Watching the movement
going this way and that
putting your feet
into the water
moving out deeper
swimming farther
seeing where the tides
take you
The magic of the ocean
makes me come alive again
as if from a dream
no matter how far away
you come back again
to the edge of everything

1. https://unsplash.com/@m_gatus?utm_source=medium&utm_medium=referral

2. https://unsplash.com?utm_source=medium&utm_medium=referral

Hope springs from fear
the shine of the sun
the feel of the water
the touch of the sand
shells, animals, palm trees
the beach is where
I feel at home
and yet so often
far from that home
Far from the great, wise mother
to which we all return
I have traveled far
across the globe
to find myself
to find an answer
to questions
I dare not ask
in the silence
of my soul
Great, wise mother
guide me home

When Grief Comes Flooding Back

Photo by Diana Parkhouse[1] on Unsplash[2]
Funeral for a friend

I'm never going to see again
didn't know that last time
would be our last
or I would have asked you
to stay a little longer
have another drink
or some dinner with us
We didn't know
that you were going to go
away from us so soon
you were young still
I thought we had years
but we didn't
just a few months
and we moved away
Your last days
didn't have us in them
and I regret
the lost time
spent elsewhere
We didn't know
that you would go
away so soon
Didn't know we would never
see your face or your smile again
didn't know we would never
hear you laugh again
or tell another story
or give me a hug goodbye
There is a hole in my heart

---

1. https://unsplash.com/@ditakesphotos?utm_source=medium&utm_medium=referral

2. https://unsplash.com?utm_source=medium&utm_medium=referral

where your face used to be
it has torn a hole in me
to lose you so soon
You should have had a long life
we lost you too young
you were still so vibrant
so alive
so seemingly strong
we didn't know something
was badly wrong
How do you let go
of someone you have lost?
how do you move on
when you see a reminder
in so many things that happen
and you are on my mind again
you are in my heart always
my dear friend
You were like a brother to me
that is what we called each other
brother and sister
We shared so many times together
good times with good music
and bad times when one of us cried
now I am crying alone
because my brother has died
and I can't let go
can't seem to see you
as an angel up above
but I dream of you still
and think of your love
You were there for me

when no one else was
you listened to me cry
and picked me up off the floor
So many days
and nights shared
so many times
so much fun
so much life
You were always full of life
you always made the party shine
I don't know how you could go
lost so much before your time
You were too young to go
and you still have a piece
of me and my heart
and so many other hearts
so many friends
who lift a glass in memory
It is the coming of the ship
for your Viking funeral
I can see in my mind's eye
Ready to build your pyre
and send you off to Valhalla
Will I see you again one day?
on some distant shore
where those ships land
and I will come home
and find you on the sand
waiting for my ship
when it comes in at last
I think I will see you
I think we will meet again

in another life somewhere
when the hourglass turns
But today you are gone
my dear friend and brother
I will never forget you
there is no other
just like you were
a unique and shining star
They ask if you would rather
burn out or fade away
I guess you burned too brightly
and then you burned out
I miss you today
I missed you yesterday too
maybe one day my heart will heal
until then I just feel
all of this pain inside
wishing to be made whole
But there is this space
inside my soul
where you used to be
when you were here
right beside me
Death doesn't hurt for you
not for the one who dies
you move on to the
otherworld
Death hurts for those
loved ones left behind
and I just wonder
how long it takes hearts
to mend

to find some peace
without my dear friend

Whispers of the Universe

© Taiga[1] | Megapixl.com[2]

1. https://www.megapixl.com/taiga-stock-images-videos-

Lately I have been listening
to whispers of the universe
as I learn to silence the mind
silence all the chatter
of the world in my ears
I want to learn to listen
more closely
to those whispers
Telling me to love more
to be more open in my heart
to have more compassion
to have forgiveness
for the past and all
that has come before
Things sometimes get so loud
we don't hear those little whispers
telling us that there is hope still
that there is love and beauty
for all of us in the world
The world is a beautiful place
and the universe is vast
and full of so much possibility
full of so much hope and love
full of wonderous beauty
I hear those quiet, angelic whispers now
Singing in my ear
telling me it will all be alright
that I can live the life
that I have always dreamed
and life is so much more

---

portfolio

2. https://www.megapixl.com/

than what it has seemed
for such a long while to be
I can do anything
see anything
be anything
dream of anything
and have it come true
That is what the whispers say
they say come with me and dance
this vast dance that is all life
that is made of love and light
and our own aliveness
inside all of what happens
No matter the past
we are still alive now
we still have this chance
to wake up every day
and do something different
We can embrace life
we can learn the dance
this is what the whispers say
they say come out here
with me and learn to play

You Can't Change the Past

Photo by Marcos Paulo Prado[1] on Unsplash[2]

Looking backward
with regret
instead of looking forward
is no way to live
and yet we do
so much of the time
Feeling trapped
by choices made

1. https://unsplash.com/@marcospradobr?utm_source=medium&utm_medium=referral
2. https://unsplash.com?utm_source=medium&utm_medium=referral

promises spoken
how do we fix
what the past has broken?
So much life left
and yet it feels like sometimes
just a slow march
towards our demise
Stop living in regret
stop living in the past
turn your face
to the sunshine
once again
instead of facing backward
towards the shadows
face forward
towards the future
The future is where
happiness and possibilities
wait for you
whispering with hope
and promise
of a better tomorrow
a better today
You can't unmake your choices
but you can make something new
something beautiful
out of the broken pieces
of this ruined life
Being ruined and broken
doesn't have to last forever
There is always a new day
filled with new hope

and new promise
and you can do something
different or better
for yourself
Stop looking backward
there is nothing for you
back there in the shadows
only pain
broken dreams
and so much fear
Stop letting the past define you
there is so much yet for you to do

Your Life is a Blank Slate

Your life is a blank slate
still to be written
sometimes wiped clean
to start again
What would you make
what would you write
or draw
design or make
Your life is yours
open and full of possibilities
space to write
all of your dreams
What would you dream?
what would you be?
always remember
you are free
Do what you want
be who you want

make something new
as beautiful as you
It is never too late
to dream a new dream
never too late
to wipe the slate clean
Start anew and fresh
a blank canvas
a new sheet of paper
a blank white screen
to write your new life
What will you write?
what will you be?
what stories do you have
still left to tell
Start again
start fresh
with this new day
each morning new
each day alive
a chance for love
a chance for freedom
you only have to see it
What do you crave
in the depths of your soul?
what will it take
to make your life whole?
This is what you do
that is where you go
to the land of your dreams
to the place of your heart
Near or far

inside your heart
that is where dreams live
that is your song
still to be sung
It is never too late
you still have today
so start the day strong

Your Shadow

Image by Engin Akyurt[1] from Pixabay[2]

You don't have to run
from your shadow self
she is part of you
and can't be denied

1. https://pixabay.com/de/users/engin_akyurt-3656355/?utm_source=link-attribution&utm_medium=referral&utm_campaign=image&utm_content=2359562
2. https://pixabay.com/de/?utm_source=link-attribution&utm_medium=referral&utm_campaign=image&utm_content=2359562

she is these feelings
hiding inside
Turn around not just
to face her
but to embrace her
bring her in close again
love her
cherish her
make her part of you again
She is always there
always a part of you
always waiting
for you to turn round
for you to face her
Your shadow is there
cast backwards from the sun
its sunset rays
caressing your face
and she grows taller
as darkness nears
She is of the moon
and of the stars
but remember
you can't have darkness
you can't have a shadow
without a little light
She is swallowed
in the total darkness
of the blackest night
invisible
part of a bigger shadow
cast across everything

As you walk the darkness
she is with you too
only hiding
and you just see yourself
and your inner darkness
you being of light
goddess of the day
let her be
your lady of the night
stop fighting her
let her take her place
by your side
Face towards the shadow
away from the sun
walk another way
and see where the path leads
Your light means nothing
without your darkness
it is the contrast
that gives you your spark
that makes you alive
with the fire of the night
you used to shine
Somehow like Alice
you have lost your 'muchness'
and I wonder was she
your shadow self
what gave you that muchness
a richness
that you can't find in the sun
only in the stillness of moonlight
Maybe the truth is

that you used to be the shadow
and she the one who cast it
and somehow
you became confused
on who was who
Maybe there is no difference
between you and she
Maybe we are all half darkness
half light
and we let these halves war
instead of letting them combine
like yin and yang
we are the teardrop
and the dragon's fang
both and neither
living shades of gray
but we deny it
longing for the light
for our goodness only
and we deny our night
We make ourselves smaller
we make ourselves less
trying to fit
into a daytime world
when ours is of twilight
of midnight
and trying to make ourselves
fit in their world
the world of light
was misguided at best
plain wrong at worst
We are not just our goodness

we are more
there is life in darkness too
there is movement in silence
and we look at the stars
we dream another dream
The night is a time
for lovers too
to find their beds
to find each other
Maybe we can't be lovers
the same way by daylight
only in the shadows
maybe you need to see
the moonlight on my face
to calm your fears
erase your tears
So shall I come to you in moonlight
in the space of your dreams
dark shadow of my former self
remembered in this shrouded night
Remember who you are
who you used to be
you used to be the shadow
dance like her now

Don't miss out!

Visit the website below and you can sign up to receive emails whenever Nicole Dake publishes a new book. There's no charge and no obligation.

https://books2read.com/r/B-A-RYPWC-YAPJF

Also by Nicole Dake

Trauma Survivor's Guide to Coping With Panic Attacks
Happy. Healthy. Rich. The smart mom's guide to living your best life.
A Dream of Becoming
A Narcissist Destroyed My Life
Trauma Survivor's Guide to Coping With Panic Attacks UK Edition
How to Self-Publish Your E-Book
Facing Heartbreak
Compassion is the Ultimate Goal of Spirituality

Watch for more at https://medium.com/@nicoledake.

About the Author

Nicole Dake is a blogger, author, and mom of two. Nicole blogs about parenting with a focus on health & wellness for moms and kids. Nicole has a BA in Psychology with a minor in Religious Studies from University of Colorado, Paralegal Certification from Boston University.

Nicole is also a Spiritual Life Coach and ordained minister of the Universal Life Church Monastery.

Visit my blog at: https://medium.com/@nicoledake

Read more at https://medium.com/@nicoledake.

www.ingramcontent.com/pod-product-compliance
Lightning Source LLC
LaVergne TN
LVHW041017150826
845672LV00001B/120

* 9 7 9 8 2 3 0 2 4 0 1 1 2 *